TABLE OF CONTENTS

INTRODUCTION

CHAPTER 1

INTRODUCTION TO RDBMS AND SQL
WHAT IS A DATABASE?
RELATIONAL DATABASE MANAGEMENT SYSTEMS (RDBMS)
WHY USE DATABASES?
INTRODUCTION TO SQL

CHAPTER 2

CREATING DATABASES AND DEFINITION TABLE RELATIONSHIPS
ENTITY RELATIONSHIP DIAGRAM (ERD)
CREATING A DATABASE
DELETING A DATABASE
CREATING A TABLE
TABLE RELATIONSHIPS

CHAPTER 3

PERFORMING CRUD OPERATIONS

CREATING DATA
SELECTING DATA
UPDATING DATA
DELETING DATA

CHAPTER 4

FILTERING WITH OPERATORS, SORTING WITH ORDER BY
SQL OPERATORS
THE WHERE CLAUSE
ORDER BY CLAUSE

CHAPTER 5

AGGREGATE FUNCTIONS
GROUP BY CLAUSE
HAVING CLAUSE

CHAPTER 6

UNDERSTANDING TABLE JOINS
INNER JOIN
LEFT JOIN
RIGHT JOIN
FULL JOIN
JOINING THREE OR MORE TABLES
UNION

CHAPTER 7

SUB-QUERIES
WITHOUT SUB-QUERIES
USING SUB-QUERY

CHAPTER 8

CONSTRAINTS IN SQL
NOT NULL
UNIQUE
PRIMARY KEY
FOREIGN KEY
INDEX
DEFAULT
CHECK

CHAPTER 9

STORED PROCEDURES IN SQL
ADVANTAGES OF STORED PROCEDURES IN SQL
CREATING A STORED PROCEDURE
EXECUTING A STORED PROCEDURE
STORED PROCEDURE FOR INSERTING RECORDS
STORED PROCEDURE FOR UPDATING RECORDS
STORED PROCEDURE FOR DELETING RECORDS
MODIFYING A STORED PROCEDURE

DELETING A STORED PROCEDURE

CHAPTER 10

SQL TRIGGERS
TRIGGER SYNTAX
AFTER TRIGGER
INSTEAD OF TRIGGER

CHAPTER 11

TRANSACTIONS IN SQL
WHAT IS A TRANSACTION?
PROBLEM WITH TRANSACTIONS
SOLUTION WITH TRANSACTIONS
CUSTOM TRANSACTION ROLLBACK

CHAPTER 12

DEADLOCKS IN SQL
DUMMY DATA CREATION
PRACTICAL EXAMPLE OF DEADLOCK
DEADLOCK ANALYSIS AND PREVENTION
SOME TIPS FOR DEADLOCK AVOIDANCE

CHAPTER 13

SQL Cursors

CHAPTER 14

FUNCTIONS IN SQL
BUILT-IN FUNCTIONS
DATENAME FUNCTION EXAMPLE
USER DEFINED FUNCTIONS

CHAPTER 15

DATABASE NORMALIZATION
DATA REDUNDANCY PROBLEM
SOLUTION IS NORMALIZED DATABASE
DATABASE NORMAL FORMS

CHAPTER 16

SQL TEMPORARY TABLES
CREATING TEMPORARY TABLE
GLOBAL TEMPORARY TABLES
TEMPORARY TABLES AND STORED PROCEDURE

CONCLUSION

this document, including, but not limited to, — errors, omissions, or inaccuracies.

Introduction

The book "Title Here" is aimed novice as well as advanced database professionals. In this book I have explained all the concepts that are required for developing a real world database system. The concepts have been explained with the help of an imaginary "Hospital" database system that stores records of patients, doctors, examinations and patients. After reading this book, you should be able to develop real world databases of your own. All the examples in this book have been executed on MS SQL Server 2017; though you can use any database server you want as most of the queries remain same. Finally, I would advise you to practice these queries as you study them. This will help you understand the concepts better. You will make mistakes but you will learn better.

Chapter 1

Introduction to RDBMS and SQL

What is a Database?

There are two parts of a computer application: Logic, which is implemented in the form of code functions and data, upon which the functions act to perform some task. When an application is being executed, it stores data in RAM (Random Access Memory). However RAM is volatile media which means as soon as you close the application the data is wiped out of the RAM. A persistent storage media is required to store data.

Computer's hard disk is a persistent storage media. One approach is store data on files in the hard disk. In fact file based storage systems were used in the early days of computers. However storing and managing data with files is a cumbersome task. Especially for huge and complex and data, file based systems are not suited. A more sophisticated and refined approach is required to handle such data. This is where Database Management Systems (DBMS) come to play.

DBMS are persistent storage systems that employ sophisticated techniques to store manage, access and manipulate data. Different DBMS systems store data in different formats. DBMS that stores data in the form of related tables are called Relational Database Management Systems RDBMS, which is the most widely used DBMS. DBMS are also commonly known as Database Systems. Classic textbooks of database define database systems as follows:

"A collection of information stored in a computer in such a way that it can be easily accessed , managed and manipulated"

Relational Database Management Systems (RDBMS)

This book is about SQL, which is the language used to interact with RDBMS. Therefore it is imperative to study some basic RDBMS concepts.

There are five basic components of RDBMS.

- Table
- Columns
- Fields
- Primary Key
- Foreign Key

Table

A database table is used to store data in the form of rows and columns. This is similar to real world data tables which consist of rows and columns. Usually a database table corresponds to real world entity. For instance if you are developing a database for a hospital it can have entities such as patient, doctor, treatment, medicine, wards etc. In your database you can use tables to store record for each of these entities. Let's take a look at a patient's table.

Id	Name	Gender	Age	Blood_Group	Phone
1	Wan	Male	41	O+	45126985
2	Joe	Male	23	B+	14564895
3	Jen	Female	32	AB-	12478956
4	Liz	Female	27	B+	25416348
5	Sam	Male	19	A-	13479563

Table 1.0: An example of Patient's Table

Table 1.0 contains patients' information such as its Id, Name, Gender, Age, Blood Group and Phone.

Rows

Each row in the database table contains record of one instance of the entity. You can see that there are multiple rows in the patient's table. Here each row contains record of one patient. No two rows can have record of one patient.

Columns

A table column store information about particular attribute of the entity. For instance, if you look at the Table 1.0, each column contains values that correspond to a particular patient attribute. The Name column contains names of the patient, similarly the age column stores information about patients' ages.

Primary Key

Primary key is used to uniquely identify records within a table. The column that contain primary key is called primary key column. Each value in the primary key column should be unique. No two or than two records can have same value for their primary key column. In Table 1.0 the Id column is the primary key column.

Foreign Key

Foreign keys are used to create relationship between two tables. Foreign key column contains values from the primary key column of some other table.

We will discuss relationships in detail in the next chapter. Brief explanation is given in this section. Let's create another table and call it Patient_Treatment. This table contains information about different treatments that a patient has undergone. A patient can have multiple treatments. However one record in the Patient_Treatment table belongs to one person. This is a one to many relation between Patient and Patient_Treatment table. To implement this relation a foreign key is added to Patient_Treatment table. This foreign key refers to the primary key of the Patient table. Let's see how the Patient_Treatment should look like:

Id	Treatment	Result	Price	Patient_ID
1	Chest XRay	Both lungs functional	500	2
2	Ultrasound	Not Pregnant	750	3
3	HIV	Negative	1000	5

Table 1.1: Patient_Treatment table

In the Patient_Treatment table, the Patient_ID column is the foreign key column and it references the Id column of the Patient table. The Patient_ID column can have no value that doesn't exist in the Id column of Patient table.

Why Use Databases?

- Database foster data integrity, which means you have consist data throughout the database. Data is updated at one place and the change is reflected in all the related tables.
- Databases ensure that no redundant data is stored in the database. This is another way to ensure data integrity.
- Databases provide controlled access to data, which improves data security.
- Database streamlines the process of data creation, access and management.

Introduction to SQL

A database application has two parts: Front end or commonly referred to as user interface and backend which consists of code that interact with the database. A standard communication protocol is required to communicate with the database and perform tasks like data creation, deletion, selection and update. Structured Query Language (SQL) is that protocol or commonly referred as "language" that is used to interact with a database. SQL is a scripting language which means that SQL code is not required to be compiled before execution.

SQL Query

SQL query is a command or instruction that performs some operation on the database.

SQL is further divided into two main categories:

Data Definition Language (DDL)

Data definition is a set of queries that are used define database schema. DDL includes queries used to create, update, delete, and modify database and tables. Table 1.3 contains DDL queries along with their description

Query	Description
CREATE	Used to create new table or database
DROP	Used to delete tables or database
ALTER	Used to modify existing databases or tables

TRUNCATE	Removes all the table data and the space that hold the data.
RENAME	Used to rename a database or table
COMMENT	Adds comments to a database. (Comment is the script that is not executed and provides information about the script)

Table 1.3: DDL queries

Data Manipulation Language (DML)

DML is a set of queries that deal with the actual data within the database. DML performs task like creating, deleting, updating and selecting data from a database table. Table 1.4 contains DML queries.

Query	Description
INSERT	Used to insert data inside a table
UPDATE	Used to update existing data inside a table
DELETE:	Used to delete records from a table
SELECT:	Selects data from a table

This chapter provided a brief introduction to relational databases and SQL. In the next chapter we will write our first SQL query. We shall create a simple database and will see different types of relationships between tables.

Chapter 2

Creating Databases and Definition Table Relationships

In this book we will follow a step by step approach to explain different SQL concepts. We shall start with Entity Relationship Diagram (ERD) which serves as blue print for the database. ERD defines database scheme. We will then create our database according to that scheme. The next step will be to add some data in the database. Once we have a database with some data in it we are good to experiment with it. So let's start with ERD

Entity Relationship Diagram (ERD)

ERD is the graphical representation of database scheme. ERD contains tables in the database, the columns within those tables and relationships between the tables.

The database that we are going to develop in this book is a Hospital database. It will contain six tables: Patients, Treatment, Doctors Examinations, Patient_Examination and Patient_Visits. Figure 2.1 contains ERD for the hospital database.

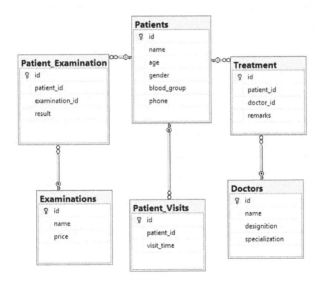

Figure 2.1: ERD for Hospital Database

The Hospital database ERD contains all the tables in the hospital database along with their relationship. These relationships will be explained later in this chapter.

Creating a Database

We have an ERD, now we must actually create our database as defined by ERD. Let's execute our first query of the book. This query will create database on the database server.

```
CREATE DATABASE Hospital;
```

The syntax of CREATE database query is very simple, you have to use the keyword CREATE DATABASE followed by the name of the database. You can give any name to your database.

Note:

It is also important to mention here that SQL is case insensitive. It is also worth mentioning that we are using MS SQL Server 2017 as our DBMS in this book. You can use any other relational database system such as MySQL, SQL Lite etc. The core SQL is similar for all the databases with only slight variations.

You could write the above query as follows:

```
Create database Hospital;
```

There will be no difference.

Deleting a Database

To delete existing database we use DROP DATABASE query. For instance if you want to delete Hospital database that we created, execute the following query:

```
DROP DATABASE Hospital;
```

Before moving forward, recreate the Hospital database if you have deleted it, since in the next section we are going to create tables within the Hospital database.

Creating a Table

We have created Hospital database but it is empty at the moment. There is no data in the database. Databases store data in tables. Therefore the first step after creating database is to create tables.

As a rule of thumb, create all the independent tables first and then the dependent tables. A table is independent if does not contain any foreign key and vice versa. The relationships between the tables define dependency and independency of tables.

If we look at the ERD Patients, Doctors and Examinations tables are independent table because they do not contain any foreign key. Therefore we will create these tables first. The syntax for creating a table is as follows:

```
CREATE TABLE table_name
(
        Colum1_name data_type constraints,
        Colum2_name data_type constraints,
)
```

Now let's create Patients table using this syntax. Execute the following query on your database server to create Patient table.

```
USE Hospital;

CREATE Table Patients
(
        idint IDENTITY (1,1) PRIMARY KEY
NOT NULL,
        name VARCHAR (50) NOT NULL,
        ageint NOT NULL,
        gender VARCHAR (50) NOT NULL,
        blood_group VARCHAR (50),
        phone BIGINT
);
```

The first line in the above query is USE Hospital. The USE command is used to specify the database in which you are creating your database. We are creating Patients table inside the Hospital database, therefore mentioned it via USE command.

Look how we defined columns inside the Patients table. To define a column we start with the column name, followed by the type of the data stored by the column and the constraints upon the key column. For instance the first column inside the Patients is the 'id' column. This column has data type of int which means that it can store integer type data (We will see data types in detail in next chapter). The third part of the column definition is the constraint specifications. A constraint implements certain rules on table columns. The id column has three constraints:

- IDENTITY: That data will be automatically added to this column starting from one and it will be incremented by 1 for each new record.
- PRIMARY KEY: Specifies that this column is the primary key column?
- NOT NULL: Column cannot hold null values

Notice that the columns in the Patients table corresponds to those defined for the Patient table in the ERD.

Similarly create Doctors and Examinations tables using following queries:

```
USE Hospital
CREATE Table Doctors
(
        idint  IDENTITY  (1,1)  PRIMARY  KEY
NOT NULL,
```

```
         name VARCHAR (50) NOT NULL,
         designition VARCHAR (50),
         specialization VARCHAR (50),

);


USE Hospital
CREATE Table Examinations
(
         idint  IDENTITY  (1,1)  PRIMARY  KEY
NOT NULL,
         name VARCHAR (50) NOT NULL,
         priceint NOT NULL,

);
```

We have created all the three independent tables. The next step is to create dependent tables i.e. Patient_Examination, Treatments and Patient_Visits table. These tables are bound in a relationship to the Patients table. Before creating these tables, let us first study the type of relationships that database tables can have.

Table Relationships

There are three major types of relationships between tables in a relational database:

- One to One Relation
- One to Many Relation
- Many to Many Relation

One to One Relation

In a one to one relation, for a record in the first table, there can be one and only one record in the related or dependent table. A simple example of one to relation is the relation between patient and his contact info. A patient can have one contact info, while particular contact info belongs to one patient. One to one relations are avoided in most of the cases and the tables participating in one to one relation are merged together. For instance you can have patient info e.g. name, last name, date of birth and contact info e.g. phone, address, email in a single table.

One to Many Relation

In one to many relation, each record in the first table can be referenced by multiple records in the second table. For instance in our Hospital database, Patients and Patient_Visits tables have one to many relationships with each other. For each record in the Patients table, there can be multiple records in the Patient_Visits table. In simple terms, a patient can have multiple visits to a hospital; however one visit belongs to only belongs to one Person.

To implement one to many relation in the database, we have to add a foreign key in the table that is on the "many" side of the relationship. This foreign key references the primary key of the table that is on the "one" side of the relationship. In the case of Patients and Patient_Visits tables, the latter will have a foreign key column that references the primary key of the former table. Let's implement it using a query.

```
USE Hospital
CREATE Table Patient_Visits (
```

```
          idint IDENTITY(1,1) PRIMARY KEY NOT
NULL,
          patient_idint      FOREIGN       KEY
REFERENCES Patients(id),
          visit_time DATETIME NOT NULL
);
```

The above script creates Patient_Visits table in the Hospital database. It also implements one to many relationship between Patient and Patient_Visits table. Take a look at the following line of code from the above script:

```
patient_idint   FOREIGN   KEY   REFERENCES
Patients(id),
```

This creates a foreign key column patient_id in the Patient_Visits table. This column references the id column of the Patients table. This is how we actually implement one to many relationships in the database.

Many to Many Relation

In many to many relation, each record in the first table can be referenced by multiple records in the second table. Similarly each record in the second table can be referenced by multiple records in the first table. For instance one patient can have multiple examinations; similarly one examination can be undertaken by multiple patients. In other words, for each record in the Patients table, there can be multiple records in the Patient_Examination table and vice versa.

Many to many relations are usually broken down into two one to many relations using a junction table. Both the tables involved in the many to many relation have one to many relation with the junction table. Junction table has foreign keys from all the tables involved in many to many relation. In the ERD for Hospital table we have defined Patient_Examination table as junction table to implement one to many relation between Patients and Examinations table. This Patient_Examination table will have two foreign keys: One that references the primary key column of the Patients table and the other that references the primary key column of the Examinations table. The following script creates Patient_Examination table in the hospital database.

```
CREATE Table Patient_Examination(

        idint IDENTITY(1,1) PRIMARY KEY NOT
NULL,
        patient_idint      FOREIGN      KEY
REFERENCES Patients(id),
        examination_idint   FOREIGN   KEY
REFERENCES Examinations(id),
        result VARCHAR(50)
);
```

Similarly Patients and Doctors also have one to many relation between them since a patient can be treated by many doctors and one doctor can treat many doctors. Here Treatments table is the junction table that implements the relation between Patient and Doctors table. The script for creating Treatments table is as follows:

```
CREATE Table Treatment(

        idint IDENTITY(1,1) PRIMARY KEY NOT
NULL,
        patient_idint        FOREIGN        KEY
REFERENCES Patients(id),
        doctor_idint FOREIGN KEY REFERENCES
Doctors(id),
        remarks VARCHAR(50)
);
```

And with this query, we have created our database and tables as defined by the ERD in Figure 2.1. In the next chapter we will perform four primary DML operations on our database.

Chapter 3

Performing CRUD Operations

In previous chapter, we created Hospital database. Now is time to perform CRUD operations on the database. CRUD is abbreviation of Create, Read, Update and Delete. These are the four most fundamental database operations. In this chapter we will see how to perform these operations.

Creating Data

To create data inside a table the INSERT query is used. The syntax for insert query is as follows:

```
INSERT   INTO   TABLE   (Column1,   Column2,
Column3 …. Column N)
```

```
VALUES (Value1, Value2, Value3 …. Value N),
(Value1, Value2, Value3 …. Value N),
(Value1, Value2, Value3 …. Value N)
```

The syntax for insert query is simple; you have to use keywords INSERT INTO TABLE followed by a pair of parenthesis. Inside the parenthesis you have to specify comma separated list of the columns where you want to insert the data. Next VALUES keyword is used followed by a pair of parenthesis that contain comma separated list of values that are to be stored in the columns. You can store multiple records at once. Each set of columns should be separated by others via commas. It is important to mention that sequence of columns and values should be similar.

If you do not specify the columns within the parenthesis after the INSERT INTO TABLE keywords, the default table scheme is used.

Let's insert some data into our Hospital database. As with the table creation, first you should insert the records to the tables that do not have any foreign key. We will start with the Patients table. Take a look at the following query:

```
USE Hospital;
INSERT INTO Patients
```

```
VALUES    ('Tom',     20,     'Male'    ,'O+',
123589746),
('Kimer', 45,'Female', 'AB+', 45686412),
('James', 16,'Male', 'O-', 78452369),
('Matty', 43,'Female', 'B+', 15789634),
('Sal', 24,'Male', 'O+', 48963214),
('Julie', 26,'Female', 'A+', 12478963),
('Frank', 35,'Male', 'A-', 85473216),
('Alex', 21,'Male', 'AB-', 46971235),
('Hales', 54,'Male', 'B+', 74698125),
('Elice', 32,'Female', 'O+', 34169872)
```

In the above query we inserted records of 10 random patients in the Patients table. Here we did not specify the column names; therefore the default column sequence will be used. The values are inserted according to the default column sequence. By default, id is the first column of the Patients. However it has Identity constraint, therefore we do not need to add any value for the id. It will be automatically added. The second column is the name column. The first value will be inserted in this column. Be careful, the name column only accepts string type data. So you must insert string. To create string, enclose the value inside single quotes. Similar, age is the second column of the Patients table and it is of integer data type therefore we enter number as second value in our insert statement.

In the same way, let's insert data into Examinations and Doctors table. The following query inserts data in the Examinations table.

```
USE Hospital;

INSERT INTO Examinations

VALUES('XRay', 750),
('Ultrasound', 600),
('LFT', 800),
('RFT', 900),
('HIV', 500)
```

Similarly, let's insert some records in the Doctor's table.

```
USE Hospital;

INSERT INTO Doctors

VALUES('Orland', 'MS', 'Nephrology'),
('Mark', 'HOD', 'Pathology'),
('Evens', 'Professor', 'Cardiology'),
('John','Demonstrator', 'Pediatrician'),
('Fred', 'DMS', 'Neurology')
```

We have added data to all the independent tables, now let's some data to the Patient_Visits table. It has a foreign key columpatient_id. This column references the id column of the Patients table. This means that patient_id column of Patient_Visits table can only have values that exist in the id column of the Patients table. In Patients table, the id column has values between 1-10. We will randomly insert these values in the patient_id column.

The following script inserts some random records in Patient_Visits table.

```
USE Hospital;

INSERT INTO Patient_Visits

VALUES(1, '19-Apr-2012'),
(2, '19-May-2012'),
(4, '25-Feb-2013'),
(6, '30-Nov-2014'),
(2, '21-Sep-2015'),
(3, '10-Oct-2011'),
(7, '01-Jan-2010'),
(9, '25-May-2012'),
(4, '17-Nov-2012'),
(8, '08-Sep-2016'),
(3, '19-Jan-2013'),
(10, '20-May-2011'),
(3, '17-Feb-2012'),
(7, '19-Mar-2014'),
(10, '05-May-2015'),
(8, '14-Feb-2011'),
(6, '29-Nov-2016'),
(10, '18-May-2010'),
(9, '09-Jun-2015'),
(8, '08-Sep-2014')
```

Now let's insert dummy records to the Treatments and Patient_Examinations table. Treatments table has two foreign key columns patient_id and doctor_id. The former references the id column of Patients table and while the latter references the id column of the Doctors table. So while inserting records for these foreign key columns we should insert only those values that exist in the corresponding referenced columns. The following script inserts record in the Treatment table.

```
USE Hospital;
INSERT INTO Treatment

VALUES (1,3, 'Fit'),
(1,3, 'Good condition'),
(2,5, 'Needs more treatment'),
(1,4, 'Referred for XRay'),
(8,1, 'Medicnes recommended'),
(5,2, 'Fit'),
(9,3, 'Perfect')
```

In the same way, execute the following script to add data to Patient_Examination table

```
USE Hospital
INSERT INTO Patient_Examination

VALUES (1,3, 'Positive'),
(1,3, 'Negative'),
(2,5, 'Positive'),
(1,4, 'Negative'),
(8,1, 'Positive'),
(5,2, 'Negative'),
```

```
(9,3, 'Positive')
```

SELECTING DATA

We have inserted data in all of our tables. Now is the time to retrieve that data. To do in SQL, we use SELECT query. You can either select data from all the columns or data from individual columns. The syntax for both operations is as follows:

Selecting all columns

```
SELECT * FROM Table_Name
```

Selecting Individual Columns

```
SELECT   column1,   column2,   column3   ...
columnN FROM Table_Name
```

Let's select all the records from the Patients table. Execute following query:

```
SELECT * FROM Patients
```

This query will retrieve all records with all column values from Patients table. The result of the above query will look like this:

id	name	age	gender	blood_group	phone

1	Tom	20	Male	O+	123589746
2	Kimer	45	Female	AB+	45686412
3	James	16	Male	O-	78452369
4	Matty	43	Female	B+	15789634
5	Sal	24	Male	O+	48963214
6	Julie	26	Female	A+	12478963
7	Frank	35	Male	A-	85473216
8	Alex	21	Male	AB-	46971235
9	Hales	54	Male	B+	74698125
10	Elice	32	Female	O+	34169872

For instance if you want to retrieve only the name, and blood_group columns for all the records in the Patients table, you can execute following query.

```
SELECT name, blood_group FROM Patients
```

The result set will look like this:

name	blood_group
Tom	O+
Kimer	AB+
James	O-
Matty	B+
Sal	O+
Julie	A+

Frank	A-
Alex	AB-
Hales	B+
Elice	O+

Updating Data

To update existing table data, the UPDATE query is used. The syntax of the update query looks like this:

```
UPDATE Table_Name
SET Column_Name = Value
```

Let's increase the price of all the examinations by 10%. To do so we have to update the value of the price column of the Examinations table by multiplying it with 1.1. The following update query performs this operation.

```
UPDATE Examinations
SET price = price * 1.1
```

Deleting Data

DELETE query is used to delete records from a table. The syntax of DELETE query is as follows:

```
DELETE FROM Table_Name
```

To delete all the records from Patient_Visits table, execute following query. (Do not forget to reinsert records in the Patient_Visits table. We will use this data to perform queries in the upcoming chapter)

```
DELETE FROM Patient_Visits
```

In this chapter we learned to create, insert, update and delete table records. However we saw that these operations are being performed on all the records. What if we want to delete only specific records? For instance what we will do if want to update records of only female patients? In the next chapter we will see how to filter data in different ways using various SQL operators and WHERE clause.

Chapter 4

Filtering with Operators, Sorting with ORDER BY

In this chapter we are going to see, how we can filter data using different types of SQL operators in conjunction with the WHERE clause.

SQL Operators

There are four major types of operators in SQL:

- Comparison Operators
- Conjunctive Operators

- Logical Operators
- Negation Operators

The WHERE Clause

Before studying SQL operators in detail, first we need to understand WHERE clause. The WHERE clause filters records based on the operator used in the query. The syntax of WHERE clause is simple. Let's see a simple example of WHERE clause. This query filters all those patient records where id is greater than 5.

```
SELECT * FROM Patients
WHERE id > 5
```

The output of the above query is as follows:

name	age	gender	blood_group	phone
Julie	26	Female	A+	12478963
Frank	35	Male	A-	85473216
Alex	21	Male	AB-	46971235
Hales	54	Male	B+	74698125
Elice	32	Female	O+	34169872

Now, let's study each SQL Operator in detail.

Comparison Operators

SQL comparison operators can be further divided into six types. These operators filter records by comparing values of the operands.

- Equality (=)
- Non-equality (<>)
- Less Than Values (<)
- Greater Than Values (>)
- Less than equal to (<=)
- Greater than equal to(>=)

The working principle of each of these operators has been demonstrated by examples. Take a look at them.

Equality Operator (=)

```
SELECT * FROM Patients
WHERE name = 'Frank'
```

The above query returns record of the patient named 'Frank'.

Non-Equality (!=)

```
SELECT * FROM Patients
WHERE name != 'Frank'
```

The above query returns records of all the patients except the one named 'Frank'.

Less Than (<)

```
UPDATE Examinations
SET price = price * 1.1
```

```
WHERE price < 250
```

The above query updates the price column of those records in the Examinations table where price is less than 250.

Greater Than (>)

```
SELECT * FROM Patients
WHERE id > 5
```

Less than Equal To (<=)

```
SELECT * FROM Patients
WHERE age <= 30
```

The above query selects all the records from Patients table where age is less than or equal to 30. The output of the above query will look like this:

id	name	age	gender	blood_group	phone
1	Tom	20	Male	O+	123589746
3	James	16	Male	O-	78452369
5	Sal	24	Male	O+	48963214
6	Julie	26	Female	A+	12478963
8	Alex	21	Male	AB-	46971235

Greater than Equal To (>=)

```
SELECT * FROM Patients
WHERE age >= 30
```

The above query selects all the records from Patients table where age is greater than or equal to 30. The output of the above query will look like this:

id	name	age	gender	blood_group	phone
2	Kimer	45	Female	AB+	45686412
4	Matty	43	Female	B+	15789634
7	Frank	35	Male	A-	85473216
9	Hales	54	Male	B+	74698125
10	Elice	32	Female	O+	34169872

Conjunctive Operators

In the previous examples we used only one operator to filter data. If we want to filter records that satisfy multiple conditions, we can use Conjunctive operators. There are two commonly used conjunctive operators in SQL.

- AND

- OR

Let's see both of them in action:

AND

```
SELECT * FROM Patients
WHERE age > 30 AND gender = 'Female'
```

The above query will retrieve records of all the patients with age greater than 30 and gender Female. The output of the above query will look like this:

id	name	age	gender	blood_group	phone
2	Kimer	45	Female	AB+	45686412
4	Matty	43	Female	B+	15789634
10	Elice	32	Female	O+	34169872

OR

```
SELECT * FROM Patients
WHERE age > 30 OR gender = 'Female'
```

This query will select records of all patients with either age greater than 30 or gender Female. The output of the above query will be:

id	name	age	gender	blood_group	phone
2	Kimer	45	Female	AB+	45686412
4	Matty	43	Female	B+	15789634
6	Julie	26	Female	A+	12478963
7	Frank	35	Male	A-	85473216
9	Hales	54	Male	B+	74698125
10	Elice	32	Female	O+	34169872

Logical Operators

Following are the most commonly used logical operators in SQL:

- IN
- BETWEEN
- LIKE
- DISTINCT
- IS NULL

IN

The IN operator is used to filter records based on the values specified in the IN operator. The IN operator takes comma separated values inside parenthesis as input. For instance if you want to retrieve records of all the patients whose blood group is O+ or O-, you can use IN operator as follows:

```
SELECT * FROM Patients
WHERE blood_groupIN('O+','O-')
```

The output of the above query will be records of all the patients with blood group O+ or O- as shown below:

id	name	age	gender	blood_group	phone
1	Tom	20	Male	O+	123589746
3	James	16	Male	O-	78452369
5	Sal	24	Male	O+	48963214
10	Elice	32	Female	O+	34169872

BETWEEN

BETWEEN operators filter records that falls between specified ranges. The range is specified using AND operator. For instance if you want to retrieve records of all the patients with id between 3 and 7, you can use BETWEEN operator as follows:

```
SELECT * FROM Patients
WHERE id BETWEEN 3 AND 7
```

The output of the above query will look be:

id	name	age	gender	blood_group	phone
3	James	16	Male	O-	78452369
4	Matty	43	Female	B+	15789634
5	Sal	24	Male	O+	48963214
6	Julie	26	Female	A+	12478963
7	Frank	35	Male	A-	85473216

LIKE

Like operator fetches records based on string matching. For instance if you want to select records of all patients whose name starts with 'J', you can use LIKE operator. The LIKE operator uses two wild cards for string matching. They are denoted by a percentage sign (%) and underscore sign (_). The % wild card specifies any number of characters whereas _ specifies only one character. So, if you want to fetch records of all the patients where name starts with J, you can use like operator as follows:

```
SELECT * FROM Patients
WHERE name LIKE('J%')
```

Here you can see we use % wild card. Here 'J%' means that the name should start with J and after that there can be any number of characters. The output of this query will be:

id	name	age	gender	blood_group	phone
3	James	16	Male	O-	78452369
6	Julie	26	Female	A+	12478963

Similarly, if you want to select all the records where 'a' is the second character in the name, you can use '_' wildcard as follows:

```
SELECT * FROM Patients
WHERE name LIKE('_a%')
```

Here '_a%' specifies that there can be one and only one character before character 'a' and after that there can be any number of characters. The output of this query will look like this:

id	name	age	gender	blood_group	phone
3	James	16	Male	O-	78452369
4	Matty	43	Female	B+	15789634
5	Sal	24	Male	O+	48963214

9	Hales	54	Male	B+	74698125

You can see, all the names have character 'a' in the second place.

DISTINCT

The DISTINCT selects only the distinct values from the specified column. For instance if you want to retrieve distinct patient ids from Patient_Examination table, you use DISTINCT operator as follows:

```
SELECT    DISTINCT    patient_id    from
Patient_Examination
```

IS NULL

IS NULL operator is used to retrieve those records where value for a particular column is NULL. A NULL value is used when we don't specify any value for the column. For instance if we want to retrieve records of all the patients where phone number is NULL, we can use following query:

```
SELECT * FROM Patients
WHERE phone IS NULL
```

The above query will not retrieve any record, since there is no record in the Patients table where phone is NULL.

NEGATION Operators

Negation operators reverse the value of the operators used in conjunction with it. Following are the most commonly used negation operators in SQL.

- NOT NULL
- NOT IN
- NOT BETWEEN
- NOT LIKE

Let's see each of these negation operators in action.

NOT NULL

The NOT NULL operator fetches records where the column specified in the WHERE clause has no NULL values. The following query retrieves records of those patients whose phone is not NULL.

```
SELECT * FROM Patients
WHERE phone IS NOT NULL
```

You will see all the records from the Patients table in the output since no record has NULL value in its phone column.

NOT IN

The NOT IN operator reverses the output of the IN operator. For instance if you want to retrieve records of all the patients except those with blood group O+ and O-, you can use NOT IN operator as follows:

```
SELECT * FROM Patients
WHERE blood_group NOT IN('O+', 'O-')
```

The output will look like this:

id	name	age	gender	blood_group	phone
2	Kimer	45	Female	AB+	45686412
4	Matty	43	Female	B+	15789634
6	Julie	26	Female	A+	12478963
7	Frank	35	Male	A-	85473216
8	Alex	21	Male	AB-	46971235
9	Hales	54	Male	B+	74698125

NOT BETWEEN

Similarly NOT BETWEEN operators retrieverecords that do not fall between specified ranges. To retrieve records from the Patients table where id is not between 3 and 7, you can use NOT BETWEEN operator as follows:

```
SELECT * FROM Patients
```

```
WHERE id NOT BETWEEN 3 and 7
```

The output of the above query will be:

id	name	age	gender	blood_group	phone
1	Tom	20	Male	O+	123589746
2	Kimer	45	Female	AB+	45686412
8	Alex	21	Male	AB-	46971235
9	Hales	54	Male	B+	74698125
10	Elice	32	Female	O+	34169872

NOT LIKE

Finally, the NOT LIKE operator retrieves those records that do not satisfy the criteria set by the LIKE operator. For example, the following query retrieves records of all the patients who do not have 'a' as second character in their names.

```
SELECT * FROM Patients
WHERE name NOT LIKE('_a%')
```

The above query will retrieve following records.

id	name	age	gender	blood_group	phone

1	Tom	20	Male	O+	123589746
2	Kimer	45	Female	AB+	45686412
6	Julie	26	Female	A+	12478963
7	Frank	35	Male	A-	85473216
8	Alex	21	Male	AB-	46971235
10	Elice	32	Female	O+	34169872

ORDER BY Clause

By default the data is retrieved in the order in which it was inserted. However you can sort the data according to some order. For instance you can sort the data by age, or alphabetically and so on. The ORDER BY clause is used for ordering data. Let's take a simple example of ORDER BY clause where data is sorted by age.

```
SELECT * FROM Patients
ORDER BY age
```

In the output you will see that the records will be arranged by the ascending order of age. The output will look like this:

id	name	age	gender	blood_group	phone
3	James	16	Male	O-	78452369

1	Tom	20	Male	O+	123589746
8	Alex	21	Male	AB-	46971235
5	Sal	24	Male	O+	48963214
6	Julie	26	Female	A+	12478963
10	Elice	32	Female	O+	34169872
7	Frank	35	Male	A-	85473216
4	Matty	43	Female	B+	15789634
2	Kimer	45	Female	AB+	45686412
9	Hales	54	Male	B+	74698125

By default the data is arranged in the ascending order if the sorted column is integer and in alphabetical order if the sorting is implemented via string column. However, you can reverse the output of default sorting by adding DESC after the ORDER BY clause.

The following query retrieves records from the Patients table in reverse alphabetical order.

```
SELECT * FROM Patients
ORDER BY name ASC
```

id	name	age	gender	blood_group	phone
8	Alex	21	Male	AB-	46971235

10	Elice	32	Female	O+	34169872
7	Frank	35	Male	A-	85473216
9	Hales	54	Male	B+	74698125
3	James	16	Male	O-	78452369
6	Julie	26	Female	A+	12478963
2	Kimer	45	Female	AB+	45686412
4	Matty	43	Female	B+	15789634
5	Sal	24	Male	O+	48963214
1	Tom	20	Male	O+	123589746

In this chapter we studied how we can filter records based on conditions. We also studied how to implement these conditions using operators and WHERE clause. Finally we covered how we can sort data in ascending and descending order using ORDER BY clause. In the next chapter, we will study the aggregate functions, GROUP BY clause for grouping aggregated results and HAVING clause for filtering aggregated results.

Chapter 5

Aggregate Functions

Aggregate functions in SQL operate on set of records and return aggregated result. For instance, aggregate functions can be used to find the sum of ages of all the patients in the Patients table or it can also be used to find the average of all the medical examinations from Examinations table of the Hospital database.

Note: It is important to mention here that all the example queries in this chapter have been executed on the Hospital database that we created in 2nd and 3rd chapter. If you do not have Hospital database with sample data, you may need to look back chapter two and three.

Following are some of the most commonly used aggregate functions in SQL:

   I.   SUM
   II.   AVG
   III.   MAX
   IV.   MIN
   V.   COUNT
   VI.   UPPER or UCASE
   VII.   LOWER or LCASE
   VIII. TOP

SUM

The sum function is used to calculate sum of all the values in a particular column. The following SUM function calculates sum of prices of all the records in the Examinations table.

```
USE Hospital
SELECT SUM(price)
FROM Examinations
```

AVG

The AVG function finds the average of all the values in from a particular column. The following AVG function calculates average of the ages of all the patients from the Patients table.

```
USE Hospital
SELECT AVG(age)
FROM Patients
```

MAX

The MAX function finds the largest value from a specified column. For instance if you want to find the age of the oldest patient from the Patients table, you can use MAX function as follows:

```
USE Hospital
SELECT MAX(age)
```

```
FROM Patients
```

MIN

The MIN function finds the smallest value from a specified column. For instance if you want to find the age of the youngest patient from the Patients table, you can use MIN function as follows:

```
USE Hospital
SELECT MIN(age)
FROM Patients
```

If you used the database that we created in Chapter 3, the above query should return 16.

COUNT

The count function is used to count the number of records. This function is normally used in conjunction with WHERE clause. For instance if you want to find the number of patients whose age is greater than 30, you can use COUNT function as follows:

```
USE Hospital
SELECT COUNT(id)
FROM Patients
WHERE age > 30
```

UPPER or UCASE

The UPPER function is used to convert all the values in the specified column to upper case. For instance, to convert all patient names to upper case, you can use UPPER function as follows:

```
USE Hospital
SELECT id, UPPER(name) as 'Name'
FROM Patients
```

In the output, you will see all the patient names in upper case. It is important to mention the 'AS' clause that we used in the above query. The AS clause is used to change the name of the column in the output. If you do not want to use the default column name you can use AS operator to change the column. The column name is not changed in the database. Usually the output of the aggregate function has no column name. Here you can use AS clause to set some custom name. In the above query, we set the value of the aggregate function column as 'Name'. The output of the above query will be:

id	Name
1	TOM
2	KIMER
3	JAMES
4	MATTY
5	SAL
6	JULIE
7	FRANK
8	ALEX
9	HALES

10	ELICE

LOWER or UCASE

The LOWER function is used to convert all the values in the specified column to lower case. For instance, to convert all patient names to lower case, you can use LOWER function as follows:

```
USE Hospital
SELECT id, LOWER(name) as 'Name'
FROM Patients
```

The above query will have the following output:

id	Name
1	tom
2	kimer
3	james
4	matty
5	sal
6	julie
7	frank
8	alex
9	hales
10	elice

TOP

The TOP function retrieves the first K records from a table where K is any integer. To retrieve the first 3 records from the patients table, TOP query can be used as:

```
USE Hospital
SELECT TOP 3 *
FROM Patients
```

GROUP BY Clause

The aggregate functions that we saw in the previous section operate on all the records in a table. For instance we saw how to retrieve average age of all the patients from the Patients. But what if we want to retrieve average age of patients with blood group O+ or O-? The GROUP BY clause allows us to do so. GROUP BY clause is used to execute aggregate functions that return output grouped by the columns specified by the GROUP BY clause. This is best explained with the help of an example. The following query retrieves the average age of all the patients grouped by their blood group.

```
SELECT blood_group, AVG(age) as 'Average
Age'
FROM Patients
GROUP BY blood_group
```

The output of the above query will be:

blood_group	Average Age
A-	35
A+	26

AB-	21
AB+	45
B+	48
O-	16
O+	25

From the above output we can infer that the average age of all the patients with blood group O+ is 25. Similarly the average age of patients having blood group B+ is 48 and so on.

HAVING Clause

With normal queries you can use WHERE clause for filtering data. However, with GROUP BY clause you cannot use WHERE, instead you have to use HAVING clause to filter data. For instance if you want to retrieve average age of patients with only those blood groups where average age is greater than 30, you can use GROUP BY clause in conjunction with HAVING clause as follows:

```
SELECT blood_group, AVG(age) as 'Average
Age'
FROM Patients
GROUP BY blood_group
HAVING AVG(age) > 30
```

The output of the above query will be:

blood_group	Average Age

A-	35
AB+	45
B+	48

You can see that average of only those blood groups have been retrieved where average is greater than 30.

In this chapter we studied different aggregate functions. We also studied how we can group aggregated result using GROUP BY clause and how we can filter aggregated result via HAVING clause. In the next chapter, we shall study how we can retrieve data from multiple tables using JOINs.

Chapter 6

Understanding Table JOINs

Till now, we have executed queries that retrieve data from one table. However, the Hospital database that we created in the third chapter has tables that have relationships with other tables. For instance we know that one patient can have multiple visits. What if we want to retrieve all the visits along with patient's information such as patient's name, gender and blood group etc.? If we look the Patient_Visits table we only have patient's id; how we can retrieve patient info such as name, gender etc. from this id? JOIN operations helpperform such operations. They help us retrieve data from two or more than two related tables.

There are four major types of JOINs in SQL. They are as follows:

- INNER JOIN
- LEFT JOIN
- RIGHT JOIN
- FULL JOIN

INNER JOIN

The INNER join retrieves data from both the tables where there exists a common value in the columns on which the

JOIN is being applied. This is best explained with the help of an example. Let's retrieve visit_time from the Patient_Visits table and name and gender from the related Patients table. To do so we implement INNER JOIN on the id column of the Patient_Visits table and id column of the Patients table. The INNER JOIN will retrieve only those records from both the tables where there is a common value in these columns. The following example implements such INNER JOIN.

```
SELECT          Patient_Visits.visit_time,
Patients.name, Patients.gender
FROM Patient_Visits
INNER JOIN Patients
ON Patient_Visits.patient_id = Patients.id
```

The output of the above JOIN query will be:

visit_time	name	gender
2012-04-19 00:00:00.000	Tom	Male
2012-05-19 00:00:00.000	Kimer	Female
2013-02-25 00:00:00.000	Matty	Female
2014-11-30 00:00:00.000	Julie	Female
2015-09-21 00:00:00.000	Kimer	Female
2011-10-10 00:00:00.000	James	Male

2010-01-01 00:00:00.000	Frank	Male
2012-05-25 00:00:00.000	Hales	Male
2012-11-17 00:00:00.000	Matty	Female
2016-09-08 00:00:00.000	Alex	Male
2013-01-19 00:00:00.000	James	Male
2011-05-20 00:00:00.000	Elice	Female
2012-02-17 00:00:00.000	James	Male
2014-03-19 00:00:00.000	Frank	Male
2015-05-05 00:00:00.000	Elice	Female
2011-02-14 00:00:00.000	Alex	Male
2016-11-29 00:00:00.000	Julie	Female
2010-05-18 00:00:00.000	Elice	Female
2015-06-09 00:00:00.000	Hales	Male
2014-09-08 00:00:00.000	Alex	Male

You can see that only those records are retrieved from both tables where there exists a common value in the columns being joined.

LEFT JOIN

LEFT JOIN also retrieves records from both the tables. However unlike INNER JOIN, it retrieves all the records from the left table but only those records from the right table where there exists a common value in the column on which the LEFT JOIN is being implemented. Here the left table is the name of the table that comes before the JOIN clause and right table is the table that comes after the JOIN clause.

For instance the following LEFT JOIN query retrieves all the records from Patients table but only those records from Patient_Visits table where there is a common value in the id column of the Patients table and patient_id column of the Patient_Visits table. For the records in the Patients table where there is no corresponding value in thePatient_Visits column(s), NULL value is inserted. The following query implements LEFT JOIN on Patients and Patient_Visits table.

```
SELECT    Patients.name,    Patients.gender,
Patient_Visits.visit_time
FROM Patients
LEFT JOIN Patient_Visits
ON                    Patients.id          =
Patient_Visits.patient_id
```

The output of the above query looks like this:

name	gender	visit_time

Tom	Male	2012-04-19 00:00:00.000
Kimer	Female	2012-05-19 00:00:00.000
Kimer	Female	2015-09-21 00:00:00.000
James	Male	2011-10-10 00:00:00.000
James	Male	2013-01-19 00:00:00.000
James	Male	2012-02-17 00:00:00.000
Matty	Female	2013-02-25 00:00:00.000
Matty	Female	2012-11-17 00:00:00.000
Sal	Male	NULL
Julie	Female	2014-11-30 00:00:00.000
Julie	Female	2016-11-29 00:00:00.000
Frank	Male	2010-01-01 00:00:00.000
Frank	Male	2014-03-19 00:00:00.000
Alex	Male	2016-09-08 00:00:00.000
Alex	Male	2011-02-14 00:00:00.000
Alex	Male	2014-09-08 00:00:00.000
Hales	Male	2012-05-25 00:00:00.000

Hales	Male	2015-06-09 00:00:00.000
Elice	Female	2011-05-20 00:00:00.000
Elice	Female	2015-05-05 00:00:00.000
Elice	Female	2010-05-18 00:00:00.000

You can see that all the records have been retrieved from left i.e. Patients table. Take a look at the patient named "Sal". It did not have any corresponding record in the Patient_Visitstable, therefore NULL value is displayed in the visit_time column. Only those records are retrieved from the right table i.e. Patient_Visits, where there is corresponding matching record in the Patients table.

RIGHT JOIN

RIGHT JOIN retrieves all the records from the right (2nd) table but only those records from the left(1st) table where there exists a common value in the column on which the LEFT JOIN is being implemented.

For instance the following RIGHT JOIN query retrieves all the records from Patients table but only those records from Patient_Visits table where there is a common value in the id column of the Patients table and patient_id column of the Patient_Visits table. For the records in the Patients table where there is no corresponding value in the Patient_Visits column(s), NULL value is inserted.

Notice that here we are treating Patient_Visits table as the left table and Patients table as the right table. This is reverse of the what we did in the last section. The following query implements RIGHT JOIN Patient_Visits and Patients table.

```
SELECT              Patient_Visits.visit_time,
Patients.name, Patients.gender
FROM Patient_Visits
RIGHT JOIN Patients
ON Patient_Visits.patient_id = Patients.id
```

The output of the above query looks like this:

visit_time	name	gender
2012-04-19 00:00:00.000	Tom	Male
2012-05-19 00:00:00.000	Kimer	Female
2015-09-21 00:00:00.000	Kimer	Female
2011-10-10 00:00:00.000	James	Male
2013-01-19 00:00:00.000	James	Male
2012-02-17 00:00:00.000	James	Male
2013-02-25 00:00:00.000	Matty	Female
2012-11-17 00:00:00.000	Matty	Female
NULL	Sal	Male

2014-11-30 00:00:00.000	Julie	Female
2016-11-29 00:00:00.000	Julie	Female
2010-01-01 00:00:00.000	Frank	Male
2014-03-19 00:00:00.000	Frank	Male
2016-09-08 00:00:00.000	Alex	Male
2011-02-14 00:00:00.000	Alex	Male
2014-09-08 00:00:00.000	Alex	Male
2012-05-25 00:00:00.000	Hales	Male
2015-06-09 00:00:00.000	Hales	Male
2011-05-20 00:00:00.000	Elice	Female
2015-05-05 00:00:00.000	Elice	Female
2010-05-18 00:00:00.000	Elice	Female

Full Join

Full join is the union of right and left join. It retrieves all the records from both the tables involved in join operations. If there are no common values in the joined columns, NULL value is added in the corresponding columns. Take a look at the following example:

```
USE Hospital

SELECT              Patient_Visits.visit_time,
Patients.name, Patients.gender
FROM Patient_Visits
FULL JOIN Patients
ON Patient_Visits.patient_id = Patients.id
```

The above script will fetch following records from
Hospital database.

visit_time	name	gender
2012-04-19 00:00:00.000	Tom	Male
2012-05-19 00:00:00.000	Kimer	Female
2013-02-25 00:00:00.000	Matty	Female
2014-11-30 00:00:00.000	Julie	Female
2015-09-21 00:00:00.000	Kimer	Female
2011-10-10 00:00:00.000	James	Male
2010-01-01 00:00:00.000	Frank	Male
2012-05-25 00:00:00.000	Hales	Male
2012-11-17 00:00:00.000	Matty	Female
2016-09-08 00:00:00.000	Alex	Male

2013-01-19 00:00:00.000	James	Male
2011-05-20 00:00:00.000	Elice	Female
2012-02-17 00:00:00.000	James	Male
2014-03-19 00:00:00.000	Frank	Male
2015-05-05 00:00:00.000	Elice	Female
2011-02-14 00:00:00.000	Alex	Male
2016-11-29 00:00:00.000	Julie	Female
2010-05-18 00:00:00.000	Elice	Female
2015-06-09 00:00:00.000	Hales	Male
2014-09-08 00:00:00.000	Alex	Male
NULL	Sal	Male

Joining Three or More Tables

In the previous examples of this chapter we fetch data by joining two tables. However in real world database you will need to join more than two tables. Consider the example of Hospital database. Here we know that Patients and Examinations tables have many to many relation. This relationship has been implemented via junction table Patient_Examination. Both Patients and Examination tables have one to many relation with this

Patient_Examination table. Now if we want to display all the names from the patients column along with the name of the examination that they underwent, we need to join three tables: Patients, Patient_Examination and Examinations table. To see how we can accomplish this, take a look at the following script:

```
USE Hospital

SELECT  Patients.name,  Examinations.name,
Examinations.price
FROM Patients
JOIN Patient_Examination ON Patients.id =
Patient_Examination.patient_id
JOIN            Examinations            ON
Patient_Examination.examination_id      =
Examinations.id
```

In the output you will see patients' name, examination name and examination price.

name	name	price
Tom	LFT	800
Tom	LFT	800
Kimer	HIV	500
Tom	RFT	900
Alex	XRay	750
Sal	Ultrasound	600
Hales	LFT	800

UNION

The join operator is used to retrieve records by merging columns from different tables. You can also merge data by row. For instance, you can retrieve name of patients and names of doctors in a single table merged by rows. It is pertinent to mention that the type of columns, number of columns and the order of columns for all the tables being merged should be same. Let's take a union of the id and name columns of Patients and Doctors table.

```
USE Hospital
SELECT id, name from Patients
UNION
SELECT id, name from Doctors
```

The output of the above query will be:

id	name
1	Orland
1	Tom
2	Kimer
2	Mark
3	Evens
3	James
4	John
4	Matty
5	Fred
5	Sal
6	Julie
7	Frank
8	Alex
9	Hales

10	Elice

In this chapter we studied different JOIN operations for retrieving data from multiple tables. We also saw how to merge data by rows using UNION operation. We have covered most of basics SQL concepts, from the next chapter we will start exploring complex SQL concepts. In the next chapter we will study SQL sub-queries.

Chapter 7

Sub-queries

Till now we have been executing queries that execute single operation such as inserting data, joining tables, deleting records etc. However we often come across scenarios where we have to perform multiple tasks in a single go. This is where sub-queries come handy. In simplest words, sub-query is a query within a query. But the question is, why do we need sub-queries? The answer is explained with the help of a simple scenario.

Suppose you want to retrieve the names of all the patients with age greater than the average age of all the patients. One solution is to write two separate queries. The first query retrieves the average age of all the patients and saves the result in a variable. The second query then retrieves records of all the patients with age greater than the value stored in the variable. A better solution is to make use of sub-queries. The inner query retrieves the average age of all the patients while the outer query retrieves records of all the patients with age greater than the average age.

Let's implement both the solutions:

Without Sub-queries

In this case we will write two separate queries

```
DECLARE @avgageint
SELECT @avgage = AVG(age)
FROM Patients

SELECT * FROM Patients
WHERE age > @avgage
```

In the above script we first declare an integer type variable @avgage. To declare a variable in SQL we use DECLARE clause followed by the name of the variable and the type of data that the variable will store. Notice, in SQL variable name starts with @ symbol.

In the first query of the above script, we find the average age of all the patients in the Patients table and store it in @avgage variable. We then execute another select query to retrieve records of patients with age greater than the value stored in @avgage variable. If you are using the Patients table from chapter 3, the first query will 31 (average age of patients) and the second query will retrieve records of all the patients with age greater than 31. The output of the above query will be:

id	name	age	gender	blood_group	phone
2	Kimer	45	Female	AB+	45686412
4	Matty	43	Female	B+	15789634

7	Frank	35	Male	A-	85473216
9	Hales	54	Male	B+	74698125
10	Elice	32	Female	O+	34169872

Using Sub-query

Now let's perform the exact same operations using sub-query.

```
SELECT * FROM Patients
WHERE age >
(
SELECT AVG(age)
FROM Patients
)
```

If you look at closely at the above sub-query, it also has two parts: The inner query and outer query. The inner query is:

```
(
SELECT AVG(age)
FROM Patients
)
```

The inner query retrieves average age of all the patients. The result of the inner query is fed to outer query, which then retrieves records of all the patients with age greater than the average age. The output of the above query will be the following result set:

id	name	age	gender	blood_group	phone
2	Kimer	45	Female	AB+	45686412
4	Matty	43	Female	B+	15789634
7	Frank	35	Male	A-	85473216
9	Hales	54	Male	B+	74698125
10	Elice	32	Female	O+	34169872

This chapter provides a brief introduction to SQL sub-queries. In the next chapter we will see SQL constraints.

Chapter 8

Constraints in SQL

SQL constraints are set of rules applied to database tables or columns in order to maintain database integrity and limit wrong data creation. Violation of constraint during query execution leads to automatic rollback of the query. Following are some of the most frequently used constraints in SQL:

- NOT NULL
- UNIQUE
- PRIMARY KEY
- FOREIGN KEY
- INDEX
- DEFAULT
- CHECK

Not Null

The NOT NULL constraint specifies that the column value cannot be NULL or empty. In second chapter when we created Patients table we set that the id, name, gender etc. columns are NOT NULL columns. While inserting records if you do not pass the values for these columns, system will throw an error.

Unique

Unique constraint implements a condition on table column that all the values entered in this column should be unique. Such a constraint is particularly useful for columns like Social Security Number, Passport Number etc. since these values are unique for different records.

Primary Key

The Primary Key constraint implements NOT NULL as well as UNIQUE constraint on a table column. For instance, the id columns of both the Patients and Examinations table are primary key columns. Notice that did not implement UNIQUE constraint on the id column since it was auto-increment column. When a new record is inserted for a table with an auto increment column, the value in the auto-incremented column is incremented, which is unique by default.

Foreign Key

Foreign keys are used to create relationship between two tables. Foreign key column contains values from the primary key column of some other table. For instance in the Hospital database, a patient can have multiple treatments. However one record in the Patient_Treatment table belongs to one person. This is a one to many relation between Patient and Patient_Treatment table. To implement this relation a foreign key is added to Patient_Treatment table. This foreign key refers to the primary key of the Patient table.

Index

The index constraint in SQL is similar to indexes that you find in books. A book index is used to speed up process of searching content within the book. Similarly, sql indexes are used to speed up query execution processes on certain columns. It is a common practice not to create indexes on frequently updating tables since indexes are updated along with data which slows down the process. Let's create an index on "gender" column of the Patients table.

```
USE Hospital;
CREATE INDEX pat_gender
ON Patients (gender);
```

To create an indexyou use CREATE INDEX keyword followed by the name of the index. Next, you have to specify the name of the table and column on which you want to create index.

Default

At times we want to insert some default value in a database column in case if no value is available for the column. In such scenarios we can implement default constraint on the column. The default constraint adds some default value in the column if no value is provided for that column at the time of insertion of record. The following script adds default value of "Male" in the gender column if no value is provided for that column:

```
CREATE Table Patients
(
        idint IDENTITY (1,1) PRIMARY KEY
NOT NULL,
        name VARCHAR (50) NOT NULL,
```

```
        ageint NOT NULL,
        gender   VARCHAR   (50)   NOT   NULL
DEFAULT 'Male',
        blood_group VARCHAR (50),
        phone BIGINT
);
```

Check

The check constraint is used to implement a custom
check on any table column. Suppose you want that the
price of any examination cannot be less than 100, you
can create check on price column as follows:

```
CREATE Table Examinations
(
        idint IDENTITY (1,1) PRIMARY KEY
NOT NULL,
        name VARCHAR (50) NOT NULL,
        priceint NOT NULL,
check (price >= 100)

);
```

Chapter 9

Stored Procedures in SQL

Imagine that have to execute large, complex query that performs a specific task. If you need to perform that task again, you will again have to write that large piece of script. If you are executing your queries over a network, you will have to send large amount of data over the network. This approach has several draw backs. First one is that you have to execute complex script again and again, secondly it will consume large bandwidth over the network.

A better approach is to make use of stored procedures. Stored procedure is a set of SQL statements grouped under a single heading. In this chapter, we shall see how to create, execute, modify and delete stored procedures in MS Sql Server. But before that, let us see what some of the advantages of stored procedures are.

Advantages of Stored Procedures in SQL

- **Execution Speed**

When a stored procedure is executed for the first time it is optimized, parsed, compile and stored in the local database cache. Next time when you execute the stored procedure, the compiled version is executed from cache memory which greatly improves execution speed of the stored procedures.

- **Less Network Bandwidth**

As mentioned earlier that stored procedures are compiled and stored in the cache memory. This means that large complex SQL script is sent to the database over network only once. When you want to execute the stored procedure again you only have to send the command to execute stored procedure rather than the whole script. This reduces bandwidth utilization.

- **Reusability**

Another advantage of stored procedures is its usability. Stored procedure executes set of statements. Therefore, you can write the statements once and then simple execute stored procedure whenever you want to execute those set of statements.

- **Security**

SQL stored procedures also foster security since you can restrict users from executing stored procedures while allowing them to execute other SQL statements.

Creating a Stored Procedure

It is very easy to create stored procedures in SQL. It has following syntax.

```
CREATE PROCEDURE procedure_name
AS
BEGIN
        Sql statements here ……..
END
```

To create a stored procedure, you have to use CREATE PROCEDURE command followed by the name of the stored procedure. Then you have to use AS clause followed by BEGIN and END statements. The body or the SQL statements that the procedure will execute are written inside BEGIN and END.

Now, let us create a simple stored procedure named spListPatients which lists records from the Patients table arranged in ascending order of name.

```
USE Hospital

GO --- Begins New Batch Statment

CREATE PROCEDURE spListPatients
AS
BEGIN

        SELECT * FROM Patients
        ORDER BY name
END
```

Take a look at the above script, here we started with "Use Hospital" command. This tells the database server that the stored procedure should be stored in the Hospital database. Next we use GO command to start a new batch statement. It is pertinent to mention here that CREATE PROCEDURE statement should always be the first statement in the batch. But here we have "Use Hospital" as first statement, this is why we used GO clause here.

To create the stored procedure, simply execute the above script. To see if the stored procedure has actually been created, go to following path in your SQL Server management studio:

Object Explorer -> Database -> Hospital (your DB name) -> Programmability -> Stored Procedures

The following screenshot shows this:

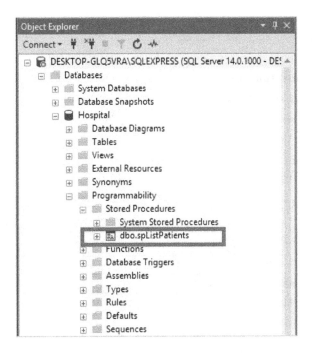

Here you can see your newly created stored procedure named "spListPatients".

Executing a Stored Procedure

To execute stored procedure we use following syntax:

```
EXECUTE stored_procedure_name
```

Yes, it is that simple. Now let us execute our spListPatients stored procedure that we created in the last section. Execute the following query:

```
EXECUTE spListPatients
```

We know that the spListPatients stored procedure retrieves records of all patients arranged in the alphabetical order of name. The output will look like this:

id	name	age	gender	blood_group	phone
8	Alex	21	Male	AB-	46971235
10	Elice	32	Female	O+	34169872
7	Frank	35	Male	A-	85473216
9	Hales	54	Male	B+	74698125
3	James	16	Male	O-	78452369
6	Julie	26	Female	A+	12478963
2	Kimer	45	Female	AB+	45686412
4	Matty	43	Female	B+	15789634
5	Sal	24	Male	O+	48963214
1	Tom	20	Male	O+	123589746

Stored Procedure for Inserting Records

We know how to create stored procedures for select statement. In this section we will see how to create stored procedure for inserting records. For this purpose, we will create parameterized stored procedures. The

following query creates a stored procedure that inserts
one record in the Patients table.

```
USE Hospital;
GO -- Begins New Batch

Create Procedure spInsertPatient
    (@Name Varchar(50), @Age int, @Gender
Varchar(50),    @Blood_Group    VARCHAR(50),
@Phone int)
As
Begin
    Insert Into Patients
    Values    (@Name,        @Age,    @Gender,
@Blood_Group, @Phone )
End
```

Take a careful look at the above script. Here after the
name of the stored procedure spInsertPatient, we
specified the list of parameters for the stored procedure.
The parameters should match the table columns in which
you are inserting the data. You can give any name and
order to these parameters but the data types of these
parameters must match the data types of the
corresponding columns. For instance the data type of the
age column in the Patients table is int, therefore the data
type of the parameter that matches this column (@Age
in this case) must also be int.

Now when you execute the above stored procedure, you
also have to pass the values for the parameters. These

values will be inserted in the database. It is pertinent to mention that type of the values passed must also match the type of the parameters. Take a look at the following script:

```
EXECUTE   spInsertPatient   'Julian',   25,
'Male', 'O+', 45783126
```

The above line executes the spInsertPatient stored procedure and inserts a new patient record in the Patients table where name of the patient is "Julian". To if new record has actually been inserted, execute the spListPatients stored procedure again. In the output you will see your newly inserted record.

Stored Procedure for Updating Records

The stored procedure for updating records is similar in syntax to that of inserting records. In this case of updating records, we create stored procedure with parameters that receive values for SET and WHERE condition. Let us take an example. The following stored procedure updatesthe age of patient named Julian.

```
USE Hospital;
GO -- Begins New Batch

Create       Procedure       spUpdatePatient
(@PatientNameVarchar(50), @PatientAgeint)
As
Begin
```

```
    Update Patients
    SET age= @PatientAge
        WHERE name = @PatientName
End
```

The following script executes the spUpdatePatient stored procedure.

```
EXECUTE spUpdatePatient 'Julian', 30
```

When you execute the above stored procedure the age of the patient named "Julian" will be updated to 30.

Stored Procedure for Deleting Records

To delete records using stored procedures, you have to write a parameterized stored procedure that accepts the value for filtering records as parameter. The following script creates a stored procedure that deletes record of the patient whose name is passed as argument to the parameter:

```
Create        Procedure        spDeletePatient
(@PatientNameVarchar(50))
As
Begin
    DELETE FROM Patients
        WHERE name = @PatientName
End
```

Now while executing this stored procedure, you have to pass the name of the patient whose record is to be deleted. The following script deletes record of the patient named "Julian".

```
EXECUTE spDeletePatient 'Julian'
```

Modifying a Stored Procedure

If you want to change the functionality of the stored procedure, you can modify it. For instance, if you want spListPatients stored procedure to retrieve all the records from Patients table in the reverse alphabetical order, you can modify it using ALTER statement. Take a look at the following script:

```
USE Hospital

GO --- Begins New Batch Statment

ALTER PROCEDURE spListPatients
AS
BEGIN

        SELECT * FROM Patients
        ORDER BY name DESC
END
```

Now if you execute the spListPatients stored procedure, you will see all the records from Patients table retrieved in reverse alphabetical order of the name. The output will look like this:

id	name	age	gender	blood_group	phone
1	Tom	20	Male	O+	123589746
5	Sal	24	Male	O+	48963214
4	Matty	43	Female	B+	15789634
2	Kimer	45	Female	AB+	45686412
6	Julie	26	Female	A+	12478963
3	James	16	Male	O-	78452369
9	Hales	54	Male	B+	74698125
7	Frank	35	Male	A-	85473216
10	Elice	32	Female	O+	34169872
8	Alex	21	Male	AB-	46971235

Deleting a Stored Procedure

To delete a stored procedure, DROP PROCEDURE statement is used. The following script deletes spDeletePatient stored procedure.

```
DROP PROCEDURE spDeletePatient
```

In the next chapter we will see SQL Triggers.

Chapter 10

SQL Triggers

Triggers in SQL are used to automatically perform an action on database when DDL or DML operation takes place. For instance, consider a scenario where you want to give discount of 10 percent on the prices of all the examination records that will be inserted in future; you can do so using triggers. Another example can be of log maintenance. You want that whenever a new record is inserted an entry is made in the log table as well. You can perform such operations with triggers.

There are two types of triggers in SQL: AFTER and INSTEAD OF triggers. The AFTER trigger is executed after an action has been performed. For instance if you want to log the operation after an operation has been performed you can use AFTER trigger. On the other hand if you want to perform a different operation in place of the actual event, you can use INSTEAD OF trigger. In this chapter we shall see example of both types of triggers:

Trigger Syntax

Trigger syntax is complex, therefore before seeing actual example, let's first understand the syntax. Take a look at the following script:

```
CREATE    [    OR    ALTER    ]    TRIGGER    [
schema_name.]name_of_trigger
ON {TABLE | VIEW }

{ FOR | AFTER | INSTEAD OF }
{ [ INSERT ] [ , ] [ UPDATE ] [ , ] [ DELETE
] }
AS
{

BEGIN

The SQL statements to execute ….

END

}
```

Now let's see what is happening in the above script, line by line. To create a trigger, the CREATE TRIGGER statement is used. To ALTER existing trigger we can use ALTER TRIGGER statement. Next the database scheme and name of the trigger is specified. After that ON TABLE clause specifies the name of the table or view. Next, you have to mention the type of trigger using FOR clause. Here you can write AFTER or INSTEAD OF. Finally you write AS BEGIN and END statements. Inside the BEGIN and END clause you write the SQL statements that you want executed when trigger fires.

AFTER Trigger

Now let's see a simple example of AFTER trigger. We will insert a new record in the Patients table of Hospital database that we created in Chapter3. When the record is inserted we will use an AFTER trigger to add an entry into the Patient_Logs table. We do not have Patient_Logs table at the moment in Hospital database. Execute the following query to create this table:

```
USE Hospital;

CREATE TABLE Patient_Logs
(
id INT IDENTITY(1,1) PRIMARY KEY,
patient_id INT NOT NULL,
        patient_name VARCHAR(50) NOT NULL,
        action_performed  VARCHAR(50)  NOT
NULL

)
```

Now we have our Patient_Logs table. Let's create our AFTER trigger that will automatically log an entry in Patient_Logs table whenever a record is inserted Patients table. Take a look at the following script:

```
USE Hospital;
GO -- begin new batch
CREATE TRIGGER [dbo].[PATIENT_TRIGGER]
ON [dbo].[Patients]
AFTER INSERT
AS
BEGIN
        SET NOCOUNT ON;

        DECLARE          @patient_id          INT,
@patient_nameVARCHAR(50)

        SELECT  @patient_id = INSERTED.id,
@patient_name = INSERTED.name
        FROM INSERTED

        INSERT INTO Patient_Logs
VALUES(@patient_id, @patient_name, 'Insert
Operation')
END
```

Here in the above script we create trigger named
PATIENT_TRIGGER on dbo database scheme. This is
AFTER type trigger and fires whenever a new record is
inserted into Patients table. In the body of the trigger
starting from BEGIN, we declared set a variable
NOCOUNT ON. This returns the number of affected rows.
Next we declared two variables @patient_id and
@patient_name. These variables will hold the id and
name of the newly inserted patient record.

The INSERTED clause here is a temporary table that holds newly inserted record. The SELECT statement is used in the script to select the id and name from the INSERTED table and store them in patient_id and patient_name variables, respectively. Finally the INSERT statement is used to insert the values in these variables to Patient_Logs table.

Now, simply insert a new record in the Patients table by executing the following query:

```
USE Hospital
INSERT INTO Patients
VALUES('Suzana',    28,    'Male',    'AB-',
65821479)
```

When the above query executes, the PATIENT_TRIGGER fires, which inserts a record in Patient_Logs table too. Now if you select records from your Patient_logs table, you will see your new log entry.

```
USE Hospital
SELECT * FROM Patient_Logs
```

The output will look like this:

id	patient_id	patient_name	action_performed
1	14	Suzana	Insert Operation

INSTEAD OF Trigger

In the previous section we created AFTER trigger which is executed after an event has occurred. In this section we will study INSTEAD OF Trigger. As mentioned earlier, the INSTEAD OF trigger executes when we want to execute an alternative action instead of executing the event that triggered the action. For instance, consider a scenario where you want to update price of different examinations. You also want to implement the condition that if price is less than 250, it should not be updated. Also, you want to keep track of all the efforts to update the price. In such case you can use INSTEAD OF trigger to execute a script which checks If the updated price is less than 250 you, log entry in to the table that "price cannot be updated", otherwise update the price and log the entry that "price updated". The following example creates this INSTEAD OF trigger.

Chapter 11

Transactions in SQL

Transactions in SQL are used to execute set of queries in Boolean fashion. This means that either all the queries in a transaction will be executed or none will execute. A transaction is declared successful if all the queries within the transaction complete their execution. In case if any query fails to execute, all the executed queries are reverted.

Consider example of Automated Teller Machine (ATM). If you want to withdraw cash from ATM, you have to perform several steps. First you have to insert your card and enter your ATM pin. Then ATM machine displays several options. You select cash withdrawal option and enter the amount. The machine deducts the money from your account and releases currency notes or the machine may first release the currency notes and then deducts the amount from your account; this depends upon implementation. However, what if machine deducts the amount from your account first and then system crashes without releasing currency notes? In such a case, the amount will be deducted from your account without you having withdrawn it.

This is extremely risky. Ideally, if a user is unable to withdraw money, the deducted amount should be transferred back to his account. In other words, either both the operations should be completed or none should complete. Transactions allow us to achieve this functionality.

What is a Transaction?

Every query in SQL is an example of transaction. For instance when you insert some records in the database using INSERT statement, you are executing a transaction with single query. If your transaction has only one query, it is treated as transaction by default. However, if you want to execute more than one query in a transaction, you have to use a particular syntax that we shall see in a few moments. Let us first try to see what happens if we try to execute a set of queries without transactions.

Problem with Transactions

Let us execute set of three queries. The first query inserts a new record in Patients table of the Hospital database, the second query updates the newly inserted record and the third query deletes the record. We shall sequentially execute these three queries in one go. We will not use transactions here to see the problem that occurs. Execute the following script.

```
USE Hospital

INSERT INTO Patients
VALUES  ('Tommy',  35,  'Male',  'B-',
62547891)

UPDATE Patients
SET age = 'Thirty Six' WHERE name = 'Tommy'

DELETE from Patients
WHERE name = 'Tommy'
```

Execute the above script. You should see the following output:

In the output, you see that 1 row was affected and then the error occurred which says that varchar value "Thirty Six" cannot be converted to the integer data type. This makes sense, since the second query updates the age column which is an integer column, therefore you cannot insert string value "Thirty Six" in this column. The database server threw an error and the script stopped executing. However, if you select the records from Patients table, you will see the record that we inserted using the first insert query as shown highlighted in the following table:

1	Tom	20	Male	O+	123589746
2	Kimer	45	Female	AB+	45686412
3	James	16	Male	O-	78452369
4	Matty	43	Female	B+	15789634
5	Sal	24	Male	O+	48963214
6	Julie	26	Female	A+	12478963
7	Frank	35	Male	A-	85473216
8	Alex	21	Male	AB-	46971235
9	Hales	54	Male	B+	74698125
10	Elice	32	Female	O+	34169872
14	Suzana	28	Male	AB-	65821479
15	Tommy	35	Male	B-	62547891

Note: Your records can be different depending upon the version of the Patients table you are using, but you should see the newly inserted records in the output.

From the output you can see that although the script terminated at second query, the first query completed its execution. But we do not want that. If the second query fails, the queries executed previously should be reverted. To do so, we can use Transactions.

Before proceeding delete the newly inserted record, since we will try to re-insert it using Transactions. Execute the following query to delete newly inserted record of patient named "Tommy":

```
DELETE from Patients
WHERE name = 'Tommy'
```

Solution with Transactions

Now, we will execute the same three queries that we executed in the last section, but this time with transactions. To create a transaction, you simply have to use BEGIN TRANSACTION statement. To mark end of transaction, use COMMIT TRANSACTION statement. The script that you want executed within the transaction should be written inside these two statements. Let us execute the insert, update and delete statements with a transaction.

```
USE Hospital
```

```
BEGIN TRANSACTION

        INSERT INTO Patients
        VALUES ('Tommy', 35, 'Male', 'B-',
62547891)

        UPDATE Patients
        SET age = 'Thirty Six' WHERE name =
'Tommy'

        DELETE from Patients
        WHERE name = 'Tommy'

COMMIT TRANSACTION
```

When you execute the above script, you will see the same output. The first query will be executed and then data type conversion error will be displayed. However, here we are executing our queries as a transaction, therefore when the second query fails; the first query will also be rolled back. That means that the insert operation performed by the first query will be reverted. Now, if you select all the patient records from Patient table, you will not find any patient named "Tommy".

Custom Transaction Rollback

In the previous section we saw that a failure to execute a query within a transaction, automatically roll backs the transaction. However, you might want to rollback a transaction manually if a certain condition is met.

Consider a scenario where you are executing a transaction that inserts a new examination record in the Examinations. You want that no two records in the table have same name. There if the table has a record with same name as the newly inserted record, the transaction should be rolled back and the record should not be inserted. Else the transaction should proceed and insert the record. Here we are manually rolling back the transaction. To do so, we simply use the following syntax.

```
ROLLBACK Transaction_name
```

In the previous section we did not give any name to the transaction. However you can also have named transactions, particularly if you want to roll it back. The named transaction can be created using this syntax:

```
BEGIN TRANSACTION Transaction_name
```

The following script inserts a new record in Examinations table. If the table contains record with same name as the newly inserted record, the transaction is rolled back; else the transaction is committed.

```
USE Hospital
DECLARE @count int
```

```
BEGIN TRANSACTION AddExamination

        INSERT INTO Examinations
        VALUES ('HCV', 900)

        SELECT   @count   =   COUNT(*)   FROM
Examinations WHERE name = 'HCV'

        IF @count > 1
                BEGIN
                        ROLLBACK
TRANSACTION AddExamination
                        PRINT  'Examination
record with same name exists already'
                END
        ELSE
                BEGIN
                        COMMIT   TRANSACTION
AddExamination
                        PRINT  'Examination
record successfully inserted'
                END
```

In the above script we insert a new examination named
"HCV" in the Examinations table. After that we count the
number of records with name "HCV" in the Examinations
table. If the number of records is greater than one, that
means we inserted duplicate records, we rollback our
transaction. Else we proceed and commit the
transaction.

If you execute the above script for the first time, you will see that the transaction will be committed and your record will be inserted. This is because at this point to time there is no examination named "HCV". You will see the following output on the console.

```
Messages
(1 row affected)
Examination record successfully inserted
```

However, if you try to execute the above script for the second time, the transaction will be rolled back since at this point of time, it has a record named "HCV" which was inserted when you executed the transaction for the first time. If you run the above script for the second time, the output will be:

```
(1 row affected)
Examination record with same name exists already
```

In this chapter we what transactions are and how they are implemented. In the next chapter we shall study another extremely interesting topic i.e. deadlocks.

Chapter 12

Deadlocks in SQL

In most of the cases, multiple users access database applications simultaneously, which means that multiple transactions are being executed on database in parallel. By default when a transaction performs an operation on a database resource such as a table, it locks the resource.

During that period, no other transaction can access the locked resource. Deadlocks occur when two or more than two processes try to access resources that are locked by the other processes participating in the deadlock.

Deadlocks are best explained with the help of an example. Consider a scenario where some transactionA has performed an operation on tableA and has acquired lock on the table. Similarly, there is another transaction named transactionB that is executing in parallel and performs some operation on tableB. Now, transactionA wants to perform some operation on tableBwhich is already locked by transactionB. Similarly, transactionB wants to perform an operation on tableA, but it is already locked by transactionA. This results in a deadlock since transactionA is waiting on a resource locked by transactionB, which is waiting on a resource locked by transactionA. In this chapter we shall see a practical example of deadlocks. Then we will see how we can analyze and resolve deadlocks.

Dummy Data Creation

For the sake of this chapter, we will create a dummy database. This database will be used in the deadlock example that we shall in next section. Execute the following script

```
CREATE DATABASE dldb;
```

```
GO

USE dldb;

CREATE TABLE tableA
(
        id INT IDENTITY PRIMARY KEY,
        patient_name NVARCHAR(50)

)

INSERT INTO tableA VALUES ('Thomas')

CREATE TABLE tableB
(
        id INT IDENTITY PRIMARY KEY,
        patient_name NVARCHAR(50)

)

INSERT INTO table2 VALUES ('Helene')
```

The above script creates database named "dldb". In the database we create two tables: tableA and tableB. We then insert one record each in the both tables.

Practical Example of Deadlock

Let's write a script that creates deadlock. Open two instances of SQL server management studio. To simulate simultaneous data access, we will run our queries in parallel in these two instances.

Now, open the first instances of SSMS, and write the following script. Do not execute this script at the moment.

Instance1 Script

```
USE dldb;

BEGIN TRANSACTION transactionA

-- First update statement
UPDATE tableA SET patient_name = 'Thomas -
TransactionA'
WHERE id  = 1

-- Go to the second instance and execute
-- first update statement

UPDATE tableB SET patient_name = 'Helene -
TransactionA'
WHERE id = 1

-- Go to the second instance and execute
-- second update statement

COMMIT TRANSACTION
```

In the second instance, copy and paste the following script. Again, do not run the Script.

Instance 2 Script

```
USE dldb;

BEGIN TRANSACTION transactionB

-- First update statement
UPDATE tableB SET patient_name = 'Helene -
TransactionB'
WHERE id  = 1

-- Go to the first instance and execute
-- second update statement

UPDATE tableA SET patient_name = 'Thomas -
TransactionB'
WHERE id = 1


COMMIT TRANSACTION
```

Now we have our scripts ready in both the transaction.

Open both the instances of SSMS side by side as shown in the following figure:

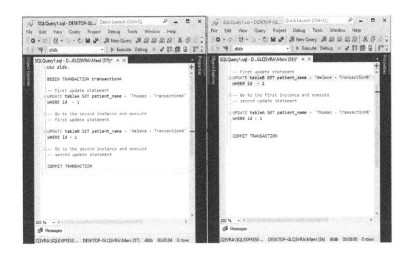

To create a deadlock we have to follow step by step approach. Go to the first instance of SQL Server management studio(SSMS) and execute the following lines from the script:

```
USE dldb;

BEGIN TRANSACTION transactionA

-- First update statement
UPDATE tableA SET patient_name = 'Thomas -
TransactionA'
WHERE id  = 1
```

In the above script, transactionA updates the tableAby setting the name of the patient with id one to 'Thomas –TransactionA'. At this point of time, transactionA acquires lock on tableA.

Now, execute the following script from the second instance of SSMS.

```
USE dldb;

BEGIN TRANSACTION transactionB

-- First update statement
UPDATE tableB SET patient_name = 'Helene -
TransactionB'
WHERE id  = 1
```

The above script executes transactionB which updates tableB by setting the name of patient with id one to 'Helene - TransactionB', acquiring lock on tableB.

Now come back again to first instance of SSMS. Execute the following piece of script:

```
UPDATE tableB SET patient_name = 'Helene -
TransactionA'
WHERE id = 1
```

Here transactionA tries to update tableB which is locked by transactionB. Hence transactionA goes to waiting state.

Go to the second instance of SSMS again and execute the following piece of script.

```
UPDATE tableA SET patient_name = 'Thomas -
TransactionB'
WHERE id = 1
```

In the above script, transactionB tries to update tableA which is locked by transactionA. Hence transactionA also goes to waiting state.

At this point of time, transactionA is waiting for a resource locked by transactionB. Similarly, transactionB is waiting for the resource locked by TransactionA. Hence deadlock occurs here.

By default, SSMS selects one of the transactions involved in the deadlock as deadlock victim. The transaction selected as deadlock victim is rolled back, allowing the other transaction to complete its execution. You will see that after few second, the transaction in one of the instances will complete its execution while an error will appear in other instance.

In the example that we just saw, transactionA was allowed to complete its execution while transactionB was selected as deadlock victim. Your result can be different. This is shown in the following figure:

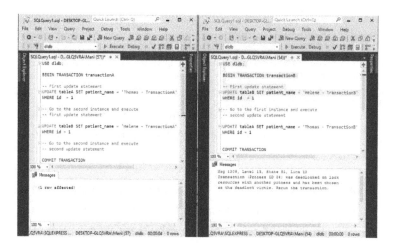

You can see the message "1 row affected" in the instance on the left that is running transactionA. On the other hand in the left instance an error is displayed that reads:

```
Msg 1205, Level 13, State 51, Line 12
Transaction (Process ID 54) was deadlocked on
lock
resources with another process and has been
chosen
as the deadlock victim. Rerun the transaction.
```

The error says that the Transaction with process ID 54 was involved in a deadlock and hence chosen as victim of the deadlock.

Deadlock Analysis and Prevention

In the previous section we generated deadlock ourselves, therefore we have information about the processes involved in the deadlock. In the real world scenarios, this is not the case. Multiple users access the database simultaneously, which often results in deadlocks. However, in such cases we cannot tell which transactions and resources are involved in the deadlock. We need a mechanism that allows us to analyze deadlocks in detail so that we can see what transactions and resources are involved and decide how to resolve the deadlocks. One such ways is via SQL Server error logs.

Reading Deadlock info via SQL Server Error Log

The SQL Server provides only little info about the deadlock. You can get detailed information about the deadlock via SQL error log. However to log deadlock information to error log, first you have to use a trace flag 1222. You can turn trace flag 1222 on global as well as session level. To turn on trace flag 1222 on, execute the following script:

```
DBCC Traceon(1222, -1)
```

The above script turns trace flag on global level. If you do not pass the second argument, the trace flag is turned on session level. To see if trace flag is actually turned on, execute the following query:

```
DBCCTraceStatus(1222)
```

The above statement results in the following output:

TraceFlag	Status	Global	Session
1222	1	1	0

Here status value 1 shows that trace flag 1222 is on. The 1 for Global column implies that trace flag has been turned on globally.

Now, try to generate a deadlock by following the steps that we performed in the last section. The detailed deadlock information will be logged in the error log. To view sql server error log, you need to execute the following stored procedure.

```
executesp_readerrorlog
```

The above stored procedure will retrieve detailed error log a snippet of which is shown below:

458	2017-11-01 15:51:47.810	spid58	Parallel redo is started for database 'test' with worke...
459	2017-11-01 15:51:47.860	spid58	Parallel redo is shutdown for database 'test' with wo...
460	2017-11-01 15:51:55.320	spid13s	deadlock-list
461	2017-11-01 15:51:55.320	spid13s	deadlock victim=process 1fcf9514ca8
462	2017-11-01 15:51:55.320	spid13s	process-list
463	2017-11-01 15:51:55.320	spid13s	process id=process 1fcf9514ca8 taskpriority=0 log...
464	2017-11-01 15:51:55.320	spid13s	executionStack
465	2017-11-01 15:51:55.320	spid13s	frame procname=adhoc line=2 stmtstart=58 stmt...
466	2017-11-01 15:51:55.320	spid13s	unknown
467	2017-11-01 15:51:55.320	spid13s	frame procname=adhoc line=2 stmtstart=4 stmte...

Your error log might be different depending upon the databases in your database. The information about all the deadlocks in your database starts with log text "deadlock-list". You may need to scroll down a bit to find this row.

Let's now analyze the log information that is retrieved by the deadlock that we just created. Note that your values will be different for each column, but the information remains same.

ProcessInfo	Text
spid13s	deadlock-list
spid13s	deadlock victim=process1fcf9514ca8
spid13s	process-list
spid13s	process id=process1fcf9514ca8taskpriority=0 logused=308 waitresource=KEY: 8:72057594043105280 (8194443284a0) waittime=921 ownerId=388813 transactionname=transactionBlasttranstarted=2017-11-01T15:51:46.547 XDES=0x1fcf8454490 lockMode=X schedulerid=3 kpid=1968 status=suspended spid=57 sbid=0 ecid=0 priority=0 trancount=2 lastbatchstarted=2017-11-01T15:51:54.380 lastbatchcompleted=2017-11-01T15:51:54.377 lastattention=1900-01-01T00:00:00.377 clientapp=Microsoft SQL Server Management Studio - Query hostname=DESKTOP-GLQ5VRA hostpid=968 loginname=DESKTOP-GLQ5VRA\Mani isolationlevel=read committed (2) xactid=388813 currentdb=8 lockTimeout=4294967295 clientoption1=671090784 clientoption2=390200
spid13s	executionStack
spid13s	frame procname=adhoc line=2 stmtstart=58 stmtend=164 sqlhandle=0x0200000014b61731ad79b1eec6740c98aab3ab91bd31af4d0000000000000000000000000000000000000000

spid13s	unknown
spid13s	frame procname=adhoc line=2 stmtstart=4 stmtend=142 sqlhandle=0x0200000080129b021f70641be5a5e43 a1ca1ef67e9721c9700000000000000000000000000 000000000000000
spid13s	unknown
spid13s	inputbuf
spid13s	UPDATE tableA SET patient_name = 'Thomas - TransactionB'
spid13s	WHERE id = 1
spid13s	process id=process1fcf9515468taskpriority=0 logused=308 waitresource=KEY: 8:72057594043170816 (8194443284a0) waittime=4588 ownerId=388767 transactionname=transactionAlasttranstarted=2017 -11-01T15:51:44.383 XDES=0x1fcf8428490 lockMode=X schedulerid=3 kpid=11000 status=suspended spid=54 sbid=0 ecid=0 priority=0 trancount=2 lastbatchstarted=2017-11- 01T15:51:50.710 lastbatchcompleted=2017-11- 01T15:51:50.710 lastattention=1900-01- 01T00:00:00.710 clientapp=Microsoft SQL Server Management Studio - Query hostname=DESKTOP-GLQ5VRA hostpid=1140 loginname=DESKTOP-GLQ5VRA\Mani isolationlevel=read committed (2) xactid=388767 currentdb=8 lockTimeout=4294967295 clientoption1=671090784 clientoption2=390200
spid13s	executionStack
spid13s	frame procname=adhoc line=1 stmtstart=58 stmtend=164 sqlhandle=0x02000000ec86cd1dbe1cd7fc97237a12

	abb461f1fc27e278000000000000000000000000000000 00000000000000
spid13s	unknown
spid13s	frame procname=adhoc line=1 stmtend=138 sqlhandle=0x020000003a45a10eb863d6370a5f993 68760983cacbf489500000000000000000000000000 000000000000000
spid13s	unknown
spid13s	inputbuf
spid13s	UPDATE tableB SET patient_name = 'Helene - TransactionA'
spid13s	WHERE id = 1
spid13s	resource-list
spid13s	keylockhobtid=72057594043105280 dbid=8 objectname=dldb.dbo.tableAindexname=PK__table A__3213E83F1C2C4D64 id=lock1fd004bd600 mode=X associatedObjectId=72057594043105280
spid13s	owner-list
spid13s	owner id=process1fcf9515468 mode=X
spid13s	waiter-list
spid13s	waiter id=process1fcf9514ca8 mode=X requestType=wait
spid13s	keylockhobtid=72057594043170816 dbid=8 objectname=dldb.dbo.tableBindexname=PK__table B__3213E83FFE08D6AB id=lock1fd004c2200 mode=X associatedObjectId=72057594043170816
spid13s	owner-list
spid13s	owner id=process1fcf9514ca8 mode=X
spid13s	waiter-list
spid13s	waiter id=process1fcf9515468 mode=X requestType=wait

The deadlock information logged by the SQL server error log has three main parts.

1- The deadlock Victim

As mentioned earlier, to resolve a deadlock SQL server selects one of the processes involved in the deadlock as deadlock victim. In the above you can see the id of process selected as deadlock victim is *process1fcf9514ca8*. You can see this value highlighted in grey in the above log table.

2- Process List

The process list is the list of all the processes involved in a deadlock. In the deadlock that we generated, two processes were involved. In the processes list you can see details of both of these processes. The id of the first process is highlighted in red whereas the id of the second process is highlighted in green. Notice that in the process list, the first process is the process that has been selected as deadlock victim too.

Apart from process id, there you can also see other information about the processes. For instance, you can find login information of the process, the isolation level of the process etc. You can see the script that the process was trying to run. For instance if you look at the first process in the process list, you can find that it was trying to update the patient_name column of the table tableA, when the deadlock occurred.

3- Resource List

The resource list contains information about the resources that were involved in the deadlock. In our example, tableA and tableB were the only two resources involved in the deadlock. You can both of these tables highlighted in blue in the resource list of the log in the table above.

Some tips for Deadlock Avoidance

From the error log we can get detailed information about the deadlock. However we can minimize the chance of deadlock occurrence if we follow these tips:

- Execute transactions in a single batch and keep them short
- Release resources automatically after a certain time period
- Sequential resource sharing
- Not allowing user to interact with the application when transactions are being executed.

This chapter presented a brief overview to deadlocks. In the next chapter, we shall see another extremely useful concept, i.e. Cursors.

Chapter 13

SQL Cursors

Cursors in SQL are used to perform row-by-row operations on data stored in tables. By default, all the SQL queries such as SELECT, UPDATE, INSERT, and DELETE treat table data as sets. It is pertinent to note that the row operations performed by cursors are extremely slow; in most of the cases join can be used in place of cursors. In this chapter, we will see a small example of how cursors are implemented in SQL.

Let us create a cursor that will iterate through all the records in the Patients table. Here you will not see performance issues, since Patients table used in this example has only 10 records. In case of tens of thousands of records, you can clearly see performance hit while using cursors. Take a look at the following example.

```
USE Hospital

DECLARE @PatientNameNVARCHAR(50)
DECLARE @PatientAge INT

DECLARE PatientCursor CURSOR FOR
SELECT name, age FROM Patients
OPEN PatientCursor
```

```
FETCH   NEXT   FROM   PatientCursor   INTO
@PatientName, @PatientAge

WHILE(@@FETCH_STATUS = 0)
BEGIN
        PRINT   'Patient   Name   =   '   +
@PatientName   +   '| Patient   Age   =   '   +
CAST(@PatientAge AS NVARCHAR(10))
        FETCH NEXT FROM PatientCursor INTO
@PatientName, @PatientAge
END

CLOSE PatientCursor
```

Take a look at the above code. Here we create two
variables @PatientName and @PatientAge variables.
Next we declare PatientCursor for the SELECT statement
that retrieves name and age of all the patients from
Patients table.

At this point of time PatientCursor holds the name and
age of all the patients. However, before using a cursor,
we first have to open it using OPEN statement. At this
point, the cursor is pointing at the top of the first row. To
move cursor to first row, the FETCH NEXT statement is
executed. In the above script the FETCH NEXT statement
retrieves the age and name of the current record from
the PatientCursor and stores it in the @PatientName and
@PatientAge variables.

To traverse through all the records in the Patients table, a while loop is used that checks if the @@FETCH_STATUS is 0 or not. If there are more rows in the cursor, the @@FETCH_STATUS returns zero. Inside the while loop, the name and age of the patient is printed and then FETCH NEXT is used to move to next row.

Finally, the CLOSED statement is used to close the cursor. The above script will retrieve following results:

```
Patient Name = Tom| Patient Age = 20
Patient Name = Kimer| Patient Age = 45
Patient Name = James| Patient Age = 16
Patient Name = Matty| Patient Age = 43
Patient Name = Sal| Patient Age = 24
Patient Name = Julie| Patient Age = 26
Patient Name = Frank| Patient Age = 35
Patient Name = Alex| Patient Age = 21
Patient Name = Hales| Patient Age = 54
Patient Name = Elice| Patient Age = 32
```

Chapter 14

Functions in SQL

Functions in SQL are similar to functions or methods in functional programming languages such as C#, C++ and Java. Functions are used for reusability and structuring your script. The task that you want to perform repeatedly can be implemented as function. The function can then be called whenever you need to perform the task.

Built-in Functions

SQL server contains several built-in functions such as Datename,Upper, Lower and other aggregate functions. To see list of built-in functions for your "Hospital" database, go to Object Explorer -> Databases -> Hospital -> Programmability -> Functions -> System Functions.

Here you can see list of all the built-in functions. Take a look at the following screen shot for your reference:

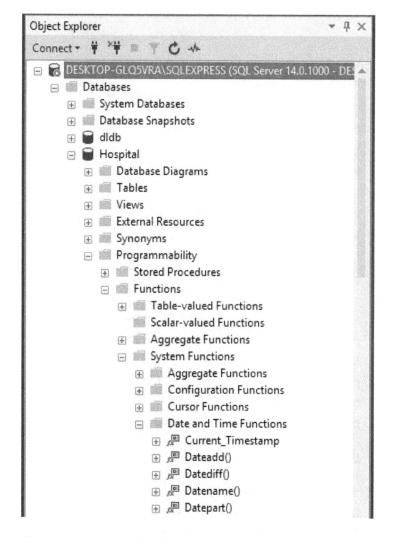

If you explore the "System Function" folder, you will see a list of functions grouped into folders according to their functionality. For example the "Date and Time Functions" folder contains list of all the date and time functions. Expanding a function displays the parameter that the function accepts and the value it returns. For instance, expand the "Datename" function. You can see that the function accepts two parameters: Date part of type varchar and Expression of type datetime. The function returns varchar value. This is shown in the following screenshot:

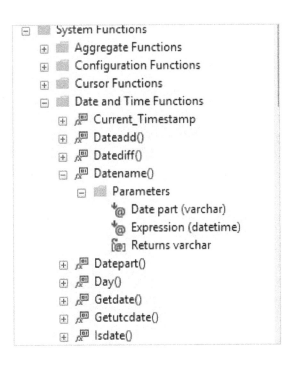

Datename Function Example

Let's see Datename Function in action. But before that, let's first create a dummy database. We will use this database for our examples in this chapter. Execute the following script:

```
CREATE DATABASE HospitalTest

USE HospitalTest
CREATE TABLE PatientTest
(
id INT IDENTITY(1,1) PRIMARY KEY,
name VARCHAR(50) NOT NULL,
gender VARCHAR(50) NOT NULL,
    DOB datetime NOT NULL,


 )


INSERT INTO PatientTest

VALUES ('Mat', 'Female', '15-MAR-1991'),
('Joe', 'Male', '03-FEB-1956'),
('Helene', 'Female', '10-MAR-1965'),
('Julie', 'Female', '25-DEC-1987'),
('Edward', 'Male', '29-SEP-1995')
```

The above script creates a new database named "HospitalTest". Inside the "HospitalTest" database a new table named "PatientTest" has been created. Some dummy records have been inserted into this table.

Now, let's see how the built-in Datename function works.

```
USE HospitalTest

SELECT    name,    DATENAME(YEAR,    DOB)    AS
YearOfBirth
FROM PatientTest
```

In the above script we pass two arguments to the Datename function: YEAR and DOB. Here the first argument is the format in which we want to retrieve the date mentioned in the second argument which is DOB in the above script. In the output you will see the name and YearOfBirth column. The former column will contain year of birth of the patient. The output of the above script will look like this:

name	BIRTH_YEAR
Mat	1991
Joe	1956
Helene	1965
Julie	1987
Edward	1995

If you pass MONTH as first parameter to DATENAME function, it will return month of the birth of the patient. You can see built-in functions are extremely helpful. However we cannot use built-in functions to perform each and every task. For instance, if we want to covert the date in this format "Sunday, March 19, 2012", we cannot do so with DATENAME function. We have to write our own script that converts the date into the desired format. To do so, we will have to call the DATENAME function multiple times with different parameters and then use string concatenation to integrate different pieces. Take a look at the following script.

```
USE HospitalTest

SELECT name, DATENAME(DW, DOB)+ ', '+
                    DATENAME(MONTH,
DOB) +', '+
                    DATENAME(DAY, DOB)+
' '+
                    DATENAME(YEAR, DOB)
AS DOB

FROM PatientTest
```

In the above we call DATENAME function four times. The first DATENAME function returns the day in words such as Sunday, the second function returns the Month in words, the third function returns the day of the month and finally the last DATENAME function returns the

YEAR. These four values are then concatenated using "+" operator to convert the date into desired format.

The output of the above script will be:

Mat	Friday, March, 15 1991
Joe	Friday, February, 3 1956
Helene	Wednesday, March, 10 1965
Julie	Friday, December, 25 1987
Edward	Friday, September, 29 1995

User Defined Functions

Though we have been to format the date according to our requirement, this technique is very crude. What if want to format the date multiple times in our script? We will have to write this chunk of script again and again. A better approach is to make use of function that accepts date in the default format and returns the date in our desired format. This is where user defined functions come handy. User defined functions are functions that perform custom functionality.

User defined functions have two parts: Function Definition and Function Call. You first have to define the script that the function will execute. Then to actually execute the script, you have to call the function.

Defining a Function

Let's create a function that accepts DATETIME type data
and returns the date in "Day, Month DD, Year" format as
we saw in the last section. Take a look at the following
script:

```
USE HospitalTest

GO


CREATE FUNCTION getFormattedDOB
  (
@Dob AS DATETIME
  )
RETURNS VARCHAR(MAX)
AS
BEGIN
        RETURN
        DATENAME(DW, @Dob)+ ', '+
        DATENAME(MONTH, @Dob) +', '+
        DATENAME(DAY,   @Dob)+ ' '+
        DATENAME(YEAR,   @Dob)
END
```

To define a function, the CREATE FUNCTION statement is
used followed by the name of the function and opening
and closing parenthesis. Inside the parenthesis, function
parameters are passed. In above script we create a
function getFormattedDOB that accepts @DOB
parameter of type DATETIME.

Next, the RETURN statement is used to specify the type of value that the function will return which is VARCHAR(MAX) in our case. Finally the script that the function executes is defined inside BEGIN and END statements. In the above script, the function retrieves Day in words, Month, Day and Year from the date passed as parameter, using the DATENAME function and then returns the concatenated value to the calling function.

Now, to see if this function has actually been created, go to Object Explorer -> Databases ->schooldb -> Programmability -> Functions -> Scalar-Valued Functions. Here you should see your newly created function. If you expand the function, you will see the parameter that the function takes. Take a look at the following screenshot for reference.

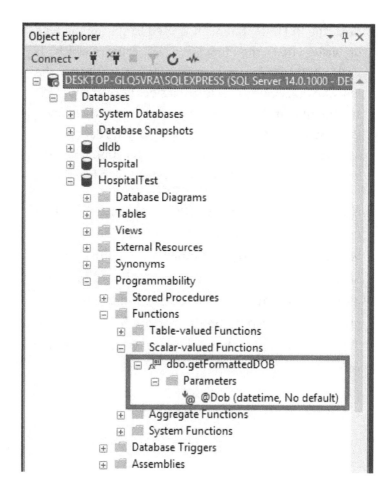

Calling the Function

Once a function has been created, you can call it as many times as you want. The syntax of calling the function is as follows:

```
[dbo].[function_name](parameters)
```

Here dbo refers to the name of the database where the function exists, function_name refers to the name of the function and parameters refer to the list of parameters that a function can accept.

Now, let's call the getFormattedDOB function that we defined in the last section:

```
USE HospitalTest
SELECT
name,
  [dbo].[getFormattedDOB](DOB) as DOB
FROM PatientTest
```

In the above script, we are calling the getFormattedDOB function inside the SELECT statement and passing it the DOB column of the PatientTest table. In the output you will see the date formatted in the desired format. The output of the above script will be:

name	DOB
Mat	Friday, March, 15 1991
Joe	Friday, February, 3 1956
Helene	Wednesday, March, 10 1965
Julie	Friday, December, 25 1987
Edward	Friday, September, 29 1995

In this chapter we studied how to use built-in functions in SQL and how to define our own functions in SQL. In the next chapter we will study Database Normalization. We will see how to normalize aun-normalize data following different rules.

Chapter 15

Database Normalization

Database normalization refers to sequential approach of organizing data to eliminate redundancy and to ensure database integrity. In this chapter we shall first see what problems we face when we have redundant data in our database. Then we will see how database normalization helps us eliminate database redundancy and ensure database integrity.

Data Redundancy Problem

In simplest words, data redundancy means data duplication. In this section we study the issue with redundant data with the help of an example. Take a look at the following table that stores records of employee. This table is not normalized and contains redundant data.

Patient Name	Patie ntAge	Patient Gender	DepN ame	Dep Hea d	NoOf Beds
Jane	45	Female	Cardi ology	Dr. Jame s	100
Mark	54	Male	Patho logy	Dr. Eliya	150

Alan	65	Male	Cardiology	Dr. James	100
Royce	21	Male	Pathology	Dr. Eliya	150
Elizabeth	27	Female	Cardiology	Dr. James	100

The above table has six columns. First three columns contain patient's information i.e. name, age and gender. The last three columns contain information about the department where patients are admitted. These columns are DepName, DepHead and NoOfBeds. If you look at the records you will find that patients Jane, Alan and Elizabeth have same values for the DepName, DepHead and NoOfBeds. This means that we have redundant data for Jane, Alan and Elizabeth. Similarly, Mark and Alan are admitted in Pathology department, therefore these two patients also have redundant data for DepName, DepHead and NoOfBeds columns.

Data redundancy leads to following issues:

1- Space Wastage

In the above table, there were only three patients with redundant values for DepName, DepHead, and NoOfBeds column. However in real world database, there can be tens of thousands of patients that are admitted in one department. In such scenarios, the values for DepName, DepHead and NoOfBeds columns will be redundant for tens of thousands of records. This requires huge disk space.

2- Data Inconsistency

Data redundancy results in data inconsistency. For instance, if the head of department for Cardiology department is changed, you will have to update all the rows in the database where department name is Cardiology. And somehow, if you miss to update a row, you will have inconsistent values for department head of Cardiology department.

3- Slow record update

The update query is slow. Suppose if there are tens of thousands of patients in the Cardiology department. If the head of department of cardiology department is changed, you will have to update tens of thousands of records. Such an update query is extremely slow.

Solution is Normalized Database

As mentioned earlier, solution to redundancy issues is normalized database. If we normalize the above table, we will have the following two tables: Patient and Department. The Patient table looks like this:

Patien tId	PatientN ame	Patient Age	PatientGe nder	Dep Id
1	Jane	45	Female	1

2	Mark	54	Male	2
3	Alan	65	Male	1
4	Royce	21	Male	2
5	Elizabeth	27	Female	1

The department table will look like this:

DepId	DepName	DepHead	NoOfBeds
1	Cardiology	Dr. James	100
2	Pathology	Dr. Eliya	150

Now let us how, the three redundancy problems have been solved using this normalized database. In the previous case, we had redundant data for DepName, DepHead and NoOfBeds columns. In the normalized database, you can see that only the DepId column of the Patient table has redundant data. Si

Similarly, inconsistency issue has also been resolved. Now if the department head of the Cardiology department is changed, you only have to make change at one place in the Department table.

Finally, since you only have to update on row, the update operation will be extremely fast.

Now, let us see how to normalize a database. We will start with our original non-normalized table and will follow step by step approach to normalize the data.

Database Normal Forms

To normalize a database, you have to achieve a particular normal form. A database is said to be in particular normal form if it adheres to specific set of rules. Database can have six normal forms denoted as 1NF, 2NF, 3NF, 4NF, 5NF, 6NF. The higher the normal form, the more a database is normalized. Most of the real world databases are in third normal form denoted as 3NF. You have to start with 1NF and then you can move to higher normal forms. In this chapter we will discuss first three normal forms as they are enough to eliminate redundancy issues.

First Normal Form (1NF)

A database in 1NF adheres to the following rules:

1- *Column Values are Atomic*

All the columns in the table should contain atomic values. This means that no column can contain more than one value in any case. Consider following table, here PatientName column contains multiple patient names.

PatientName	DepName
Jane, Alan, Elizabeth	Cardiology
Mark, Royce	Pathology

A downside to this approach is that you cannot perform CRUD operations on this database. For instance, you cannot delete record of Jane alone; you will have to delete all the records in the Cardiology department. Similarly, you cannot update the department name of Alan.

2- Repeated Column Groups are not Allowed

Repeated column groups are group of columns that have similar data. In the following table, PatientName1, PatientName2, PatientName3 columns are repeated columns since all of them store names of different patients.

Patient1Name	Patient2Name	Patient3Name	DepName
Jane	Alan	Elizabeth	Cardiology
Mark	Royce		Pathology

This approach is also not ideal since if we have to add more patient names, we will have to add more columns. Similarly, if one department has fewer patients than the other, the patient name columns for the former will have empty records which lead to wastage of storage space.

- ### Unique Identifier for Each Record

Each record in the table must have a unique identifier. A unique identifier is also known as primary key and the column that contains primary key is called primary key columns. Primary key column must have unique values. For instance, in the following table PatientId is the primary key column as values in this column.

PatientId	PatientName	PatientAge	PatientGender
1	Jane	45	Female
2	Mark	54	Male
3	Alan	65	Male
4	Royce	21	Male
5	Elizabeth	27	Female

If a database adheres to all of these conditions, it is said to be in first normal form.

Second Normal Form (2NF)

For a database to be in second normal form, it must adhere to following three conditions:

1- A database should adhere to all the conditions of the first normal form.
2- There should not be redundant data except in any column except the foreign key column.
3- Tables should be related to each other via foreign keys.

Take a look at the following table:

PatientId	PatientName	PatientAge	PatientGender	DepName	DepHead	NoOfBeds
1	Jane	45	Female	Cardiology	Dr. James	100
2	Mark	54	Male	Pathology	Dr. Eliya	150
3	Alan	65	Male	Cardiology	Dr. James	100
4	Royce	21	Male	Pathology	Dr. Eliya	150
5	Elizabeth	27	Female	Cardiology	Dr. James	100

The above table is already in first normal form since: all the values in the columns are atomic, there are no repeated column groups and each record can be identified by a primary key which is PatientId in this case.

However, the table is not in second normal form since DepName, DepHead and NoOfBeds columns have redundant values. Therefore it is not in second normal form. The solution to this problem is that the related columns that have redundant values should be grouped into a new table. We can divide the above table into two and remove redundancy problem as follows:

Patient Table

PatientId	PatientName	PatientAge	PatientGender
1	Jane	45	Female
2	Mark	54	Male
3	Alan	65	Male
4	Royce	21	Male
5	Elizabeth	27	Female

Department Table

Id	DepName	DepHead	NoOfBeds
1	Cardiology	Dr. James	100
2	Pathology	Dr. Eliya	150

Here you can see that the redundant columns such as DepName, DepHead and NoOfBeds have been grouped together in a new table. It is pertinent to mention that while grouping the columns into a table you should consider the relationship between the columns. Here PatientGender column also contained redundant values but since there was one to one relation between Patient and Gender, therefore we grouped it with Patient table. However there is one to many relation between Patient and Department table, therefore their corresponding records were grouped in Patient and Department table respectively.

Now we have two tables, the third condition of second normal form governs us to create a relationship between two tables using foreign key. Here we know that one department can have many patients. This means that we need to add a foreign key column in the Patient table that refers the Id column of the Department table. The Department table will not change; the updated Patient table will look like this:

PatientId	PatientName	PatientAge	PatientGender	DepId
1	Jane	45	Female	1
2	Mark	54	Male	2
3	Alan	65	Male	1
4	Royce	21	Male	2
5	Elizabeth	27	Female	1

In the above table, the DepId column is the foreign key column and it references the Id column of the department table!

Third Normal Form (3NF)

For a database to be in second normal form, it must adhere to the following conditions:

- The database should satisfy all the rules of the second normal form.

- There should be no column in any of the database tables that is not fully dependent upon the primary key column.

Take a look at the following table:

PatientId	PatientName	PatientAge	PatientGender	DepName	DepHead	NoOfBeds
1	Jane	45	Female	Cardiology	Dr. James	100
2	Mark	54	Male	Pathology	Dr. Eliya	150
3	Alan	65	Male	Cardiology	Dr. James	100
4	Royce	21	Male	Pathology	Dr. Eliya	150
5	Elizabeth	27	Female	Cardiology	Dr. James	100

In the above table, the DepHead and NoOfBeds columns are not fully dependent upon the primary key column PatientId. They are also dependent upon the DepName column. If the value in the DepName column changes, the values in DepHead and NoOfBeds columns also change. A solution to this problem is all the columns that depend on some column other than the primary key column, should be moved into a new table along with the column on which they depend. After that the relation between the two tables can be implemented via foreign keys as shown below:

Patient Table:

PatientId	PatientName	PatientAge	PatientGender	DepId
1	Jane	45	Female	1
2	Mark	54	Male	2
3	Alan	65	Male	1
4	Royce	21	Male	2
5	Elizabeth	27	Female	1

Department Table

Id	DepName	DepHead	NoOfBeds
1	Cardiology	Dr. James	100
2	Pathology	Dr. Eliya	150

In this chapter we studied database normalization which is one of the most important database concepts. In the last and final chapter of this book, we will study other extremely useful database concept i.e. Temporary tables.

Chapter 16

SQL Temporary Tables

Database tables can be huge with millions of records. Often times you do not need to work with all the records, rather you want to execute some operation only on subset of the records. In such cases, filtering small number of records from millions of records can be slow. Temporary tables solve this problem. Temporary tables exist in the database for a temporary period and usually contain subset of records from a permanent table. Hence, you do not have to interact with millions of records; rather you can filter required data into temporary tables and then work with temporary tables.

Creating Temporary Table

There are two ways to create temporary tables in SQL Server. We will see both of them in this section.

Creating Temporary Table without Definition

One of creating temporary tables in SQL is by using the INTO statement in conjunction with the SELECT statement. The following script creates a temporary table named #MalePatients which contains the name, age and gender of all the male patients from the Patients table.

```
USE Hospital

SELECT name, age, gender
INTO #MalePatients
FROM Patients
WHERE gender = 'Male'
```

To create temporary table, you have to first use SELECT statement to select the columns that you want in your temporary table, next you have to write INTO statement followed by table name. In the above script, the table name is #MalePatients. It is important to note that the name of temporary table always starts with #. Next we use FROM and WHERE statements to select the table and apply filters on the records, respectively.

To see where this table exists; go to "Object Explorer -> Databases -> System Databases->tempdb -> Temporary Tables". Here you will find your newly create #MalePatients temporary table. Take a look at the following screenshot:

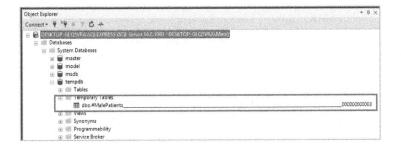

In the above screenshot, you can clearly see your newly created #MalePatients temporary table. You will find a number "000000000003" at the end of the table name. This is the unique identifier. Multiple users are accessing database at the same time and they may create temporary tables with the same name. The unique identifier helps to distinguish between two tables with the same name.

It is important to mention that by default temporary tables are only accessible to the connection that creates the table. Therefore, you can only execute queries on the temporary table via connection that created the temporary table. Now, within the same SSMS instance, execute the following query to retrieve all the records from #MalePatients table.

```
SELECT * FROM
#MalePatients
```

The output will look like this. You can see that the temporary table #MalePatients contains records of all the male patients.

name	age	gender
Tom	20	Male
James	16	Male
Sal	24	Male
Frank	35	Male
Alex	21	Male
Hales	54	Male
Suzana	28	Male

Creating Temporary Table with Definition

In the previous section we saw how to create temporary table without definition. The other method is to define temporary table first and then use it.

Open a new query window in SSMS, but keep the previous one open. We want to keep the previous connection open. Closing a query window closes the connection. Opening a new query window opens new connection. We want to keep previous connection open and create a new connection as well.

Execute the following script to create #MalePatients table by defining it first:

```
USE Hospital
```

```
CREATE TABLE #MalePatients
(
        name VARCHAR(50),
        ageint,
        gender VARCHAR (50)
)

INSERT INTO #MalePatients
SELECT name, age, gender
FROM Patients
WHERE gender = 'Male'
```

In the above script the #MalePatients temporary table
has been created just like an ordinary table and then the
INTO and SELECT statements are used to fetch records
into this table. Now if you open your Object explorer, you
will see two #MalePatients temporary table. Each
#MalePatients table will have different identifier. This is
shown in the following figure:

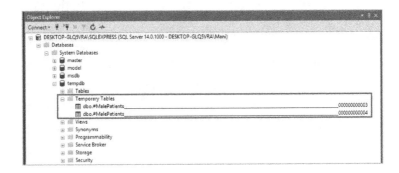

Global Temporary Tables

We can also create global temporary tables that can be accessed by all the connections, irrespective of the connection that created it. To create a global temporary table you have to start the name of the table with double hash (##). Let us create global temporary table that contains records of all the female patients from the Patients table. Take a look at the following script:

```
USE Hospital

SELECT name, age, gender
INTO ##FemalePatients
FROM Patients
WHERE gender = 'Female'
```

The above script creates ##FemalePatients global temporary table which contains the age, name and gender of all the female Patients from the Patients table.

Now you can access this ##FemalePatients table from any connection. Open a new instance of SSMS to create new instance and execute the following query:

```
SELECT * FROM ##FemalePatients
```

The above query will retrieve all the records from the ##FemalePatients table as shown below:

name	age	gender
Kimer	45	Female
Matty	43	Female
Julie	26	Female
Elice	32	Female

Deleting Temporary Tables

There are two different ways of deleting temporary tables: Automatic deletion and Manual Deletion.

Automatic Deletion:

Temporary table is deleted automatically when the connection that actually created the table is deleted. To close the #MalePatients table, simply close the SSMS query window that created the table. Global temporary tables are deleted automatically when all the connections that access the table are deleted. It is important to mention that if some query is being executed on the temporary table, the table is only deleted once the query has completed its execution.

Manual Deletion

You can manually delete a temporary table without closing the connection using following command:

```
DROP TABLE #MalePatients
```

This is similar to deleting permanent table. It is important to mention that to delete local temporary table you have to execute this query within the connection that created the table. However, to delete global temporary table, you can execute this query from any connection.

Temporary Tables and Stored Procedure

Though you cannot access a local temporary table from some other connection, you can create a stored procedure that performs some action on a temporary table inside some other connection.

For instance, create a new query window (new connection) and write the following stored procedure:

```
Use Hospital

GO
Create Procedure spInsertTempPatient
    (@Name Varchar(50), @Age int,  @Gender
Varchar(50))
As
Begin
    Insert Into #MalePatients
    Values (@Name, @Age, @Gender)
End
```

In the above script, we create a stored procedure spInsertTempPatient which inserts a new record to the #MalePatients table. Execute the above script and you will see that your stored procedure has successfully been executed. Notice that we did not create #MalePatients temporary table within the connection, yet we were able to create a stored procedure that accesses this table.

But here is the real trick. Though we can create stored procedure that accesses a temporary table within a connection that did not create it, we cannot execute stored procedure in such a connection. To execute a stored procedure, you have to be inside the connection that created the temporary table being accessed by the stored procedure.

Execute the following script inside the stored procedure that created the #MalePatients temporary table.

```
EXECUTE spInsertTempPatient 'Juana', 41,
'Male'
```

The above stored procedure inserts a new record in the #MalePatients table. Retrieve all the records from the #MalePatientstable, you will see your newly inserted record as shown below:

name	age	gender
Tom	20	Male
James	16	Male
Sal	24	Male

Frank	35	Male
Alex	21	Male
Hales	54	Male
Suzana	28	Male
Juana	41	Male

Conclusion

This book presents a high level overview of the most important SQL concepts. The book starts with basic concepts and gradually moves towards the more advanced concepts. In the book we developed an imaginary Hospital database that stores records of patients, doctors, examinations and patient visits etc. After reading this book, you should be able to design a fully functional database with all the advanced features. However, the concepts covered in this book are so vast that complete books have been written on each of them alone. Therefore, you should not stop exploring them. The best way to get better at SQL is via practice. Try to develop databases based on real world scenarios such as Airport Booking System or School Management System etc. You can use this book as a reference and develop any such database. This will help you implement situations that you face in real world. Finally, I advise you to learn other programming languages as well even if you are aiming for a career in database administration. Having good grasp of other languages will not only improve your profile, it will also help you improve your database skills. Last but not the least, work hard, stay focused and achieve your goals. Happy querying!